Careers in Serious Leisure

Leisure Studies in a Global Era

Series Editors: **Karl Spracklen**, Professor of Leisure Studies, Leeds Metropolitan University, UK; **Karen Fox**, Professor of Leisure Studies, University of Alberta, Canada

In this book series, we defend leisure as a meaningful, theoretical, and framing concept and critical studies of leisure as a worthwhile intellectual and pedagogical activity. This is what makes this book series distinctive: we want to enhance the discipline of leisure studies and open it up to a richer range of ideas; and, conversely, we want sociology, cultural geographies, and other social sciences and humanities to open up to engaging with critical and rigorous arguments from leisure studies. Getting beyond concerns about the grand project of leisure, we will use the series to demonstrate that leisure theory is central to understanding wider debates about identity, postmodernity, and globalization in contemporary societies across the world. The series combines the search for local, qualitatively rich accounts of everyday leisure with the international reach of debates in politics, leisure, and social and cultural theories. In doing this, we will show that critical studies of leisure can and should continue to play a central role in understanding society. The scope will be global, striving to be truly international and truly diverse in the range of authors and topics.

Titles include:

Brett Lashua, Karl Spracklen and Stephen Wagg (*editors*)
SOUNDS AND THE CITY
Popular Music, Place and Globalization

Oliver Smith
CONTEMPORARY ADULTHOOD AND THE NIGHT-TIME ECONOMY

Karl Spracklen
WHITENESS AND LEISURE

Robert A. Stebbins
CAREERS IN SERIOUS LEISURE
From Dabbler to Devotee in Search of Fulfillment

Soile Veijola, Jennie Germann Molz, Olli Pyyhtinen, Emily Hockert and Alexander Grit
DISRUPTIVE TOURISM AND ITS UNTIDY GUESTS
Alternative Ontologies for Future Hospitalities

Leisure Studies in a Global Era
Series Standing Order ISBN 978–1–137–31032–3 Hardback
978–1–137–31033–0 Paperback
(*outside North America only*)

You can receive future titles in this series as they are published by placing a standing order. Please contact your bookseller or, in case of difficulty, write to us at the address below with your name and address, the title of the series and the ISBN quoted above.

Customer Services Department, Macmillan Distribution Ltd, Houndmills, Basingstoke, Hampshire RG21 6XS, England

---

Careers in Serious Leisure

From Dabbler to Devotee in Search of Fulfillment

Robert A. Stebbins
University of Calgary, Canada

First published 2014 by
PALGRAVE MACMILLAN

Palgrave Macmillan in the UK is an imprint of Macmillan Publishers Limited, registered in England, company number 785998, of Houndmills, Basingstoke, Hampshire RG21 6XS.

Palgrave Macmillan in the US is a division of St Martin's Press LLC, 175 Fifth Avenue, New York, NY 10010.

Palgrave Macmillan is the global academic imprint of the above companies and has companies and representatives throughout the world.

Palgrave® and Macmillan® are registered trademarks in the United States, the United Kingdom, Europe and other countries.

ISBN 978–1–137–39972–4

This book is printed on paper suitable for recycling and made from fully managed and sustained forest sources. Logging, pulping and manufacturing processes are expected to conform to the environmental regulations of the country of origin.

A catalogue record for this book is available from the British Library.

A catalog record for this book is available from the Library of Congress.

Contents

Tables and Figures

Tables

Figures

Preface

John Berger, an English art critic, novelist, painter, and poet, once asked: "Is boredom anything less than the sense of one's faculties slowly dying?" The fulfillment career, the subject of this book, offers an antidote to the scourge of boredom, by pointing to the many opportunities to realize one's own unique gifts (faculties), talents, and character. In short, to realize one's own potential as a human being. It is probably true that most people most of the time are not bored, for this state of mind is disagreeable enough to drive them to find something more interesting to do. What they find is often only marginally better, however, if the data describing the low level of appeal of modern entertainment television (one of the world's most popular leisure activities) constitute a valid sign. Self-fulfillment is not the easiest road to happiness and well-being, but it may be argued that it is one of the most effective and surefire routes to these goals and their deepest realization.

This book, using the concept of career and the framework of the serious leisure perspective, examines the many signposts marking the fulfillment career. This career begins with an initial interest in a serious pursuit, which, if followed, leads to its efflorescence many years later in amateurism, hobbyism, volunteering, or devotee work. Years later, such careers are the stuff of autobiographies, as their authors look back on how they unfolded (e.g., Booth, 2000). This is a substantial undertaking, leaving thus little space in this book for allied considerations. That is, I cannot examine here such thorny issues as dropping out of school, being unable to afford advanced education, lacking role models in fulfilling activities, and lacking resources with which to pursue serious leisure. Nonetheless, if a person is to find a fulfilling career, there is no gainsaying that these and other antecedent conditions may be crucial.

Be that as it may, such issues have already been considered theoretically and empirically, whereas the fulfillment career spanning many years has not. Outside the field of leisure studies, developmental psychology has come closest of all disciplines to shed light on the fulfillment career. Unfortunately for the latter, however, it lacks a concept of leisure (e.g., Mannell, Kleiber, & Staempfli, 2006, pp. 112–113), thereby rendering it incapable of conceptualizing the vital role of the 'serious pursuits' (serious leisure and devotee work) in self-fulfillment and personality development. Moreover, these pursuits also serve as linchpins in the creation of optimal happiness, well-being, and positive lifestyle (e.g., Haworth, 2004; Stebbins, 2009).

Acknowledgments

I wish to thank Flora Kenson and her editorial team for their fine editorial work on this book. Every author should be so fortunate to have such fine attention given to his work.

Introduction

This book is anchored in the concept of career, as seen by the people who make decisions about the question of 'what to do with my life?' This question most commonly emerges between late adolescence and young adulthood, though it may also be pondered in mid-life and even at the time of retirement, as in 'what to do with the *rest* of my life?' Apart from the classic economic concerns of pay, health care, fringe benefits, and the like and possibly chances for promotion, many people give little careful thought to a career in either work or leisure. In fact, one of the principal themes of this book is that interest in a fulfillment career, even when it leads to deeply attractive work, originates in leisure. Here participants discover some of the deepest meanings of fulfillment. What is more, the first exposure to that leisure may be casual or serious or come through a leisure project.

People pursuing a fulfillment career are also driven by a desire to get better at their chosen leisure or work activity. 'Better' means different things to different participants. It may mean playing the trumpet better or improving at a sport. It may mean expanding a collection or creating more complex quilts. It may mean executing well more involved volunteer roles or occupational pursuits. Whatever 'better' means, it is a basic source of motivation and basic self-image of that part of life that fires the unfolding of a fulfillment career. Who am I in this world can be answered, where a fulfillment career is followed, with the observation that I am a decent (perhaps outstanding) athlete, quilter, volunteer, professional, or small business person – a respectable basis of distinction. By achieving fulfillment, participants realize their potential; they discover their unique tastes and talents for one or a few of life's many serious pursuits.

Note that the emphasis here is on leisure and work *activity*. Career fulfillment springs from doing the core activities comprising a broader general activity which are immensely rewarding (e.g., self-enrichment, self-actualization, self-expression, contributions to group effort, satisfying work with other people). In the field of career studies, research on career from this angle is rare. As Edgar Schein (2007) put it about that field, which he helped pioneer: 'there continues to be virtually no attention to the role that actual occupational experiences play in the [career] selection process' (p. 573). Still, a highly miscellaneous literature on career as anchored in core leisure and work activities does exist, though the concept of career itself is infrequently mentioned there. This book draws on a sample of this literature, some of which is quite old, to illustrate and support a variety of observations and generalizations.

The fulfillment career – which will be discussed in detail in Chapter 2 – is a passage through a set of stages of personal development in a serious pursuit. It may be conceived of both subjectively and objectively as advancement along four fundamental dimensions: effort, skill, knowledge, and experience. So how do we interest people in the serious pursuits and the self-fulfillment that comes with them once they are committed to a serious activity? The approach taken in this book to this question is to give first a detailed account of leisure studies theory bearing on the serious pursuits. This is accomplished in Chapters 1 and 2. Next, in Chapters 3 through 5, I examine closely the fulfillment career as it unfolds in the amateur, hobbyist, and volunteer activities. Chapters 6 and 7 consider those who use a serious pursuit to launch (i.e., continue) a fulfillment career in devotee work. The final chapter delves into the whys and wherefores of the long-term, if not lifelong, involvement in the serious pursuits. Fulfillment careers are deeply rewarding. They are also subject to being both constrained and facilitated by a variety of personal, social, and cultural circumstances.

1
The Serious Leisure Perspective

Serious, casual, and project-based leisure constitute the foundation of the serious leisure perspective (SLP). So far as we know in the interdisciplinary field of leisure studies, these three forms together embrace all leisure activities. The SLP is the theoretic framework that synthesizes three main forms of leisure showing, at once, their distinctive features, similarities, and interrelationships. More precisely the SLP offers a classification and explanation of all leisure activities and experiences, as these two are framed in the social psychological, social, cultural, geographical, and historical conditions in which each activity and accompanying experience take place.

The career has always been a central idea in this framework; it dates to the early studies of amateurs in archaeology, theater, and baseball (Stebbins, 1979). In principle, we could say the same for the idea of self-fulfillment, since the rewards comprising it were identified during the same research. Nonetheless, the term 'fulfillment' itself did not enter the serious pursuits' lexicon until 25 years later (Stebbins, 2004a).

Three types of leisure

As far as we know at present, all leisure may be classified as serious, casual, or project-based. It will help in the discussion that follows to have a general understanding of these three.[1] Note that this is only an introduction, however, for I will examine each much more closely later in this chapter.

The *serious* type comes in two varieties: serious leisure and devotee work. Because of their similarity, we will occasionally refer to them together as the serious pursuits. Serious leisure is the systematic pursuit of an amateur, hobbyist, or volunteer activity. It is sufficiently substantial, interesting, and fulfilling for the participant to find a career there by acquiring and expressing a combination of its special skills, knowledge, and experience. This career is experienced in free time, however, during which the individual gets better and better as an amateur, hobbyist, or volunteer. It may be necessary to persevere when, for example, mastery of a skill or idea proves elusive. And because decline is possible in these activities (e.g., athletes who are past their prime), it may also be a part of this kind of career.

Devotee work is an activity in which participants feel a powerful devotion, or, in other words, strong and positive attachment, to an occupation that they are proud to be in. In such work, the sense of achievement is high and the core activity endowed with such intense appeal that the line between this work and leisure is virtually erased. Thus one way of understanding this level of appeal is to view devotee work as serious leisure from which a full or partial livelihood is possible (for some evidence supporting this proposition, see Walker and Fenton's (2013) study of productive leisure researchers).

By contrast, *casual* leisure is immediately intrinsically rewarding and relatively a short-lived pleasurable activity. It requires little or no special training to enjoy it. It is therefore fundamentally hedonic, pursued for its significant level of pure enjoyment or pleasure. Examples are legion, including watching entertainment TV, observing scenery, drinking a glass of wine (no oenophile this imbiber), or gossiping about someone. Complexity in casual leisure increases slightly when playing a board game using dice, participating in a Hash House Harrier treasure hunt, or serving as a casual volunteer by, say, collecting bottles for the Scouts or serving tea and coffee in a religious gathering.

Project-based leisure differs in many ways from the preceding types. It is a short-term, reasonably complicated, one-off or occasional, though infrequent, innovative undertaking. But, as with the others, it is carried out in free time, or time free of disagreeable obligation. Such leisure requires considerable planning, effort, and possibly some skill or knowledge, but yet is neither serious leisure nor intended to develop into such. It is a leisure project when we volunteer to help out at an arts festival or sports event, develop the basement at home, or arrange a big celebration for a fiftieth wedding anniversary, assuming that these are not recurrent activities for the participant.

In the field of leisure studies, these three types and their subtypes are considered together under the heading of the SLP. Figure 1.1 offers a diagrammatic view of their interrelationship. It may also be viewed as a road map for our journey through this remainder of this book.

The serious pursuits

We will begin with a closer look at serious leisure and then move on to its counterpart at work. My goal for the rest of this chapter is to present enough detail about the three types to enable readers to understand how career and fulfillment are achieved in the amateur, hobbyist, and volunteer pursuits. Further, a certain amount of detail is needed to show just how critical career and fulfillment are for developing a positive lifestyle and a sense of well-being. Finally, career, in the language of the SLP, is not limited in application to remunerated work. Rather, careers both in leisure and in devotee work begin in the first, and for those who do wind up making a living at their leisure activity their careers often finish in the second. I say 'often finish', for some occupational devotees, we shall see later, find leisure in later life in applying gratis their skills and knowledge. Hence, the powerful appeal of the serious pursuit.

Serious leisure

I coined this term to express the way the people I interviewed and observed viewed the importance of these three kinds of activity in their daily lives (Stebbins, 1982). The adjective 'serious' (a word my research respondents often used) embodies such qualities as earnestness, sincerity, importance, and carefulness, rather than gravity, solemnity, joylessness, distress, and anxiety. Although the second set of terms occasionally describes serious leisure events, they are uncharacteristic of them and fail to nullify, or, in many cases, even dilute, the overall fulfillment gained by the participants. By way of example, an amateur actor loves performing theater, but battles stage fright before every performance.

Amateurs are found in art, science, sport, and entertainment, where they are invariably linked in a variety of ways with professional counterparts. The two can be distinguished economically in that the

6

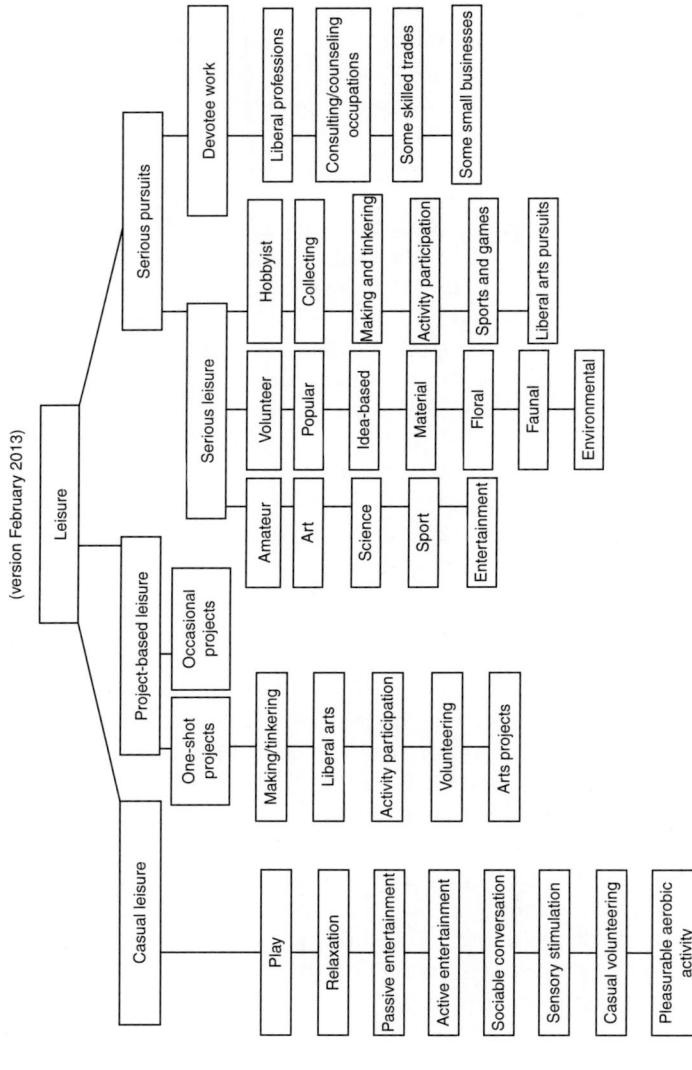

Figure 1.1 The serious leisure perspective
Source: Diagram formulated by Jenna Hartel.

activity in question constitutes a livelihood (full or part-time) for the pros but not the amateurs. The part-time professionals in art and entertainment complicate this picture; although they work part-time, their work is judged by other professionals and by the amateurs as of professional quality.

Hobbyists lack this professional alter ego, suggesting that, historically, all amateurs were hobbyists before their fields professionalized. Hobbyists can be classified in five subtypes, which we will discuss at length in Chapter 4: collectors, makers and tinkerers, noncompetitive activity participants (e.g., fishing, hiking, orienteering), hobbyists in sports and games (e.g., ultimate Frisbee, croquet, gin rummy), and liberal arts enthusiasts. The latter are enamored of the systematic acquisition of knowledge for its own sake. Many of them accomplish this by reading voraciously in a field of art, sport, cuisine, language, culture, history, science, philosophy, politics, or literature.

Volunteers perform, even for short periods of time, volunteer work in either an informal or a formal setting (Smith, Stebbins, & Dover, 2006, pp. 239–240). It is through volunteer work that these people provide a service or benefit to one or more individuals, usually receiving no pay, even though people serving in volunteer programs are sometimes compensated for out-of-pocket expenses. Moreover, in the field of nonprofit studies, since no volunteer work is involved, giving (of, say, blood, money, clothing), as an altruistic act, is not considered volunteering. Meanwhile, in the typical case, volunteers who are altruistically providing a service or benefit to others are themselves also benefiting from various rewards experienced during this process (e.g., pleasant social interaction, self-enriching experiences, sense of contributing to nonprofit group success). In other words, volunteering is motivated by two basic attitudes: *altruism* and *self-interest*. The hobbyists and the amateur, on other hand, are motivated significantly more by self-interest than by altruism.

Volitionally speaking (Stebbins, 2013a), volunteer activities are motivated, in part, by one of six types of interest: interest in activities involving (1) people, (2) ideas, (3) things, (4) flora, (5) fauna, or (6) the natural environment (Stebbins, 2007a). Each type, or combination of types, offers its volunteers an opportunity to pursue, through an altruistic activity, a particular kind of interest. Thus, volunteers interested in working with certain ideas are attracted to idea-based volunteering, while those interested in certain kinds of animals are attracted to faunal volunteering. Interest forms the first dimension of a typology of volunteers and volunteering.

But, since volunteers and volunteering cannot be explained by interest alone, a second dimension is needed. This is supplied by the SLP and its three forms. This perspective, as already noted, sets out the motivational and contextual (sociocultural, historical) foundation of the three. The intersections of these two dimensions produce 18 types of volunteers and volunteering, exemplified in idea-based serious leisure volunteers, material casual leisure volunteering (working with things), and environmental project-based volunteering (see Table 1.1).

The conception of volunteering that squares best with the leisure theme of this book is that volunteering is a distinctive type of leisure. Volunteers engage in enjoyable casual leisure, fulfilling serious leisure, or enjoyable or fulfilling project-based leisure doing activities that they may choose to accept or reject on their own terms. A key element in the leisure conception of volunteering is the feeling of not being coerced, moral, or otherwise, to participate in the volunteer activity (Stebbins, 1996).

Six distinguishing qualities

Serious leisure is further defined by six distinguishing qualities, qualities found among amateurs, hobbyists, and volunteers alike (Stebbins, 2007b, pp. 11–13). One is the occasional need to *persevere*, such as in learning how to be an effective museum guide. Yet, it is clear that positive feelings about the activity come, to some extent, from sticking with it through thick and thin, from conquering

Table 1.1   A leisure-based theoretic typology of volunteers and volunteering

Leisure interest	Type of volunteer		
	Serious leisure (SL)	Casual leisure (CL)	Project-based leisure (PBL)
Popular	SL popular	CL popular	PBL popular
Idea-based	SL idea-based	CL idea-based	PBL idea-based
Material	SL material	CL material	PBL material
Floral	SL floral	CL floral	PBL floral
Faunal	SL faunal	CL faunal	PBL faunal
Environmental	SL environmental	CL environmental	PBL environmental

adversity. A second quality is that of finding a *career* in the serious leisure role, shaped as it is by its own special contingencies, turning points and stages of achievement or involvement. Careers in serious leisure commonly rest on a third quality: significant personal *effort* based on specially acquired *knowledge, training, experience,* or *skill,* and, indeed, all four at times. Fourth, several *durable benefits,* or broad outcomes, of serious leisure have so far been identified, mostly through research on amateurs. They are self-development, self-enrichment, self-expression, regeneration or renewal of self, feelings of accomplishment, enhancement of self-image, social interaction and belongingness, and lasting physical products of the activity (e.g., a painting, scientific paper, piece of furniture). Self-gratification, or the combination of superficial enjoyment and deep fulfillment, is a further benefit and also one of the main benefits of casual leisure, where, however, the enjoyment part dominates. Of these benefits, self-fulfillment – realizing, or the fact of having realized, to the fullest one's gifts and character, one's potential – is the most powerful of all.

A fifth quality of serious leisure is the *unique ethos* that grows up around each instance of it, a central component of which is a special social world where participants can pursue their free-time interests. Unruh (1980) developed the following definition:

> A *social world* must be seen as a unit of social organization which is diffuse and amorphous in character. Generally larger than groups or organizations, social worlds are not necessarily defined by formal boundaries, membership lists, or spatial territory .... A social world must be seen as an internally recognizable constellation of actors, organizations, events, and practices which have coalesced into a perceived sphere of interest and involvement for participants. Characteristically, a social world lacks a powerful centralized authority structure and is delimited by ... effective communication and not territory nor formal group membership. (p. 277)

The sixth quality revolves around the preceding five: participants in serious leisure tend to *identify* strongly with their chosen pursuits. In contrast, casual leisure, although hardly humiliating or despicable, is nonetheless too fleeting, mundane, and commonplace for most people to find a distinctive identity there.

Rewards, costs, and motivation

The main way that the serious pursuits are set off from other kinds of work and leisure is by the extraordinary rewards they offer. These rewards act as powerful motives for being involved in one or more of those pursuits. Still, the serious pursuits are also distinguished by the fact that participants sometimes encounter costs while engaging in them. It is this profile of *rewards* and *costs* that places the serious pursuits at odds with the popular images of work as drudgery and leisure as an unalloyed good time. To repeat, this is why my interviewees kept underscoring that their leisure was out of the ordinary, not like that of most other people, they said.

The rewards of a serious leisure pursuit are the more or less routine values that attract and hold its enthusiasts. Every serious leisure career both frames and is framed by the continuous search for these rewards. Moreover, this search may take months and, in some fields, years, before the participant consistently finds self-fulfillment in his or her amateur, hobbyist, or volunteer activity. Ten rewards have so far emerged in the course of the various studies of amateurs, hobbyists, and career volunteers. As the following list shows, the rewards are predominantly personal.

Personal rewards

1. Personal enrichment (cherished experiences)
2. Self-actualization (developing skills, abilities, knowledge)
3. Self-expression (expressing skills, abilities, knowledge already developed)
4. Self-image (known to others as a particular kind of serious leisure participant)
5. Self-gratification (combination of superficial enjoyment and deep fulfillment)
6. Re-creation (regeneration) of oneself through serious leisure after a day's work
7. Financial return (from a serious leisure activity)

Social rewards

8. Social attraction (associating with other serious leisure participants, with clients as a volunteer, participating in the social world of the activity)

9. Group accomplishment (group effort in accomplishing a serious leisure project; senses of helping, being needed, being altruistic)
10. Contribution to the maintenance and development of the group (including senses of helping, being needed, being altruistic in making the contribution)

In the various studies on amateurs, hobbyists, and volunteers, these rewards, depending on the activity, were often given different weightings by research interviewees to reflect their importance relative to each other. Nonetheless, some common ground exists, for the studies do show that, in terms of their personal importance, most serious leisure participants rank self-enrichment and self-gratification as number 1 and number 2, respectively. Moreover, to find either reward, participants must have acquired sufficient levels of relevant skill, knowledge, and experience and be in a position to use these acquisitions (Stebbins, 1979; 1993a). In other words, self-actualization, which was often ranked third in importance, is also highly rewarding in serious leisure.

Let me interject here a brief aside on terminology. As mentioned earlier, I have in recent years taken to using the term *fulfillment* (Stebbins, 2004a). It points to a fulfilling experience, or more precisely, to a set of chronological experiences leading to development to the fullest of a person's gifts and character, to development of that person's full potential. Such an acquisition is certainly both a reward and a benefit of serious leisure. Rewards 1 through 3 are manifestations of fulfillment.

Satisfaction, the term I once used, sometimes refers to a satisfying experience that is fun or enjoyable (also referred to as gratifying). In another sense this noun may refer to meeting or satisfying a need or want. In neither instance does satisfaction denote the preferred sense of fulfillment just presented. In general, satisfaction is commonly what we gain from casual leisure, whereas fulfillment typically comes with its serious counterpart. Reward number 5 sometimes brings the enthusiast both, as in the jazz musician who had 'fun' at the jam session (i.e., it was fun to play well while developing further as an artist).

Both rewards and costs were mentioned by the interviewees during research into their serious pursuits. More particularly, they saw their leisure as a mix of rewards offsetting costs as experienced in the central activity. Moreover, every serious pursuit contains its own combination of these costs, which each participant must confront in some way. So far, it has been impossible to develop a general list of them, as has been done for the rewards. The reason seems to be that the costs tend to be highly specific to each activity. In general terms, the costs discovered to date may be classified as *disappointments*, *dislikes*, or *tensions*. Thus, it can be disappointing to fail to place in a sports contest, to be able to afford a treasured antique for one's collection, or paint a landscape as the artists believes it should be done. Dislikes arise in the serious pursuits when, for instance, an umpire makes what players regard as a bad call, a weekend rain spoils the backpacking trip, or a book's price discourages a hobbyist reader from purchasing it. The tensions tend to be interpersonal, as in civic orchestra conductors who lambaste the playing of a section, friction between volunteer coordinators and the volunteers whom they direct, or disagreements with the management of a recreation center that provides racket ball and badminton courts.

Interestingly, certain positive psychological states may be founded, to some extent, on particular negative, often notorious, conditions (e.g., tennis elbow, frostbite [cross-country skiing], stage fright, and frustration [in acquiring a collectible, learning a theatrical part]). Such conditions can enhance the senses of achievement and selffulfillment as the enthusiast manages to conquer the attendant adversity. People contemplating a fulfillment career need to be aware of these possibilities, recognizing especially that they are normal and that participants tend to overcome them.

Thrills and flow

Thrills are part of this framework of rewards. They are high points, the sharply exciting events and occasions that stand out in the minds of those who pursue a kind of serious leisure or devotee work. Thrills may accompany the rewards of self-enrichment and to a lesser extent those of self-actualization and self-expression. That is, thrills in serious leisure and devotee work may be seen as situated manifestations of certain more abstract rewards; they are what participants in some fields seek as concrete expressions of the rewards they find there. They are important in good part because they motivate the participant to stick with the pursuit in hope of finding similar experiences again and because they demonstrate that diligence and commitment can pay off. Because thrills, as defined here, are based on a certain level of mastery of an activity, they know no equivalent in casual leisure. The thrill of a roller-coaster ride is qualitatively different from a successful descent down a roaring rapids in a kayak where the boater has the experience, knowledge, and skill to accomplish this.

The kayaker's thrill rests on what Mihalyi Csikszentmihalyi (1990) calls the *flow* experience. The intensity with which some participants approach their leisure suggests that, there, they may at times be in psychological flow. Although many types of work and leisure generate little or no flow for their participants, those that do are found primarily in the serious pursuits of devotee work and serious leisure. Still it appears that each pursuit capable of producing flow does so in terms unique to it.

Csikszentmihalyi holds that the sensation of flow comes with actually enacting intrinsically rewarding activity. Over the years, he has identified and explored eight components of this experience:

1. sense of competence in executing the activity;
2. requirement of concentration;
3. clarity of goals of the activity;
4. immediate feedback from the activity;
5. sense of deep, focused involvement in the activity;
6. sense of control in completing the activity;
7. loss of self-consciousness during the activity;
8. sense of time is truncated during the activity.

These components are self-evident, except possibly for the first and the sixth. With reference to the first, flow fails to develop when the activity is either too easy or too difficult. To experience flow the participant must feel capable of performing what that person regards as a moderately challenging activity. The sixth component refers to the perceived degree of control the participant has over execution of the activity. This is not a matter of personal competence. Rather it is one of degree of maneuverability in confronting uncontrollable external forces. This component was well illustrated in a study of mountain hobbyists, namely, by alpinists caught in a thunder storm, kayakers paddling suddenly rising water level on a river, and snowboarders negotiating an unpredicted snowstorm on a backcountry slope (Stebbins, 2005a). Viewed through the prism of the serious pursuits, psychological flow tends to be associated with the rewards of self-enrichment and, to a lesser extent, those of self-actualization and self-expression.

Devotee work

Nearly all of what was just said about serious leisure also applies to devotee work. The chief difference is that the second is not carried out in free time. That is, it contributes significantly to the worker's livelihood.

Occupational devotees turn up chiefly, though not exclusively, in four areas of the economy. Further, devotee work there is, at most, only lightly bureaucratized. Therefore it is most common in certain small businesses, the skilled trades, the consulting and counseling occupations, and the public- and client-centered professions. Public-centered professionals serve in the arts, sports, scientific, and entertainment fields, while those that are client-centered abound in such callings as law, teaching, accounting, and medicine (Stebbins, 1992). It is assumed in all this that the work and its core activity to which people become devoted carries with it a respectable identity vis-à-vis their reference groups. For it would be difficult if not impossible to be devoted to work that those groups regarded with scorn. Still, positive identification with the job is not a defining condition of occupational devotion. Such identification can develop for other reasons, including high salary, prestigious employer, and advanced educational qualifications.

The fact of devotee work for some people and its possibility for others signals that work, as one of life's domains, can be highly positive. Granted, most workers are not fortunate enough to find such work. Even some of those in what we just called devotee occupations are not occupational devotees. That is, their work fails to meet one or more of the following six criteria (Stebbins, 2004c). To generate occupational devotion:

(1) The valued core activity must be profound; to perform it acceptability requires substantial skill, knowledge, or experience or a combination of two or three of these.
(2) The core activities must offer significant variety.
(3) The core must also offer significant opportunity for creative or innovative work, as a valued expression of individual personality.

The adjectives 'creative' and 'innovative' stress that the undertaking results in something new or different, showing imagination and application of routine skill or knowledge. That is, boredom is likely to develop only after the onset of fatigue experienced from long hours on the job, a point at which significant creativity and innovation are no longer possible.

(4) The would-be devotee must have reasonable control over the amount and disposition of time put into the occupation (the value of freedom of action), such that this person can prevent it from becoming a burden. Medium and large bureaucracies have tended to subvert this criterion. For, in interest of the survival and development of their organization, managers have felt they must deny their nonunionized employees this freedom, and force them to accept stiff deadlines and heavy workloads. But no activity, be it leisure or work, is so appealing that it invites unlimited participation during all waking hours.

(5) The would-be devotee must have both an aptitude and a taste for the work in question. This is, in part, a case of one man's meat being another man's poison. John finds great fulfillment in being a physician, an occupation that holds little appeal for Jane. Meanwhile, she adores being a lawyer (the work John finds unappealing).

(6) The devotees must work in a physical and social milieu that encourages them to pursue often and without significant constraint the core activities. This includes avoidance of excessive paperwork, caseloads, class sizes, market demands, and the like.

Sounds ideal, if not idealistic, but in fact occupations and work roles exist that meet these criteria. In today's climate of occupational deskilling, over-bureaucratization, and similar impediments to fulfilling core activity at work, many people find it difficult to locate, arrange, or maintain devotee employment.

Casual leisure

I coined the term 'casual leisure' in 1982 as part of my initial statement about serious leisure (Stebbins, 1982). At the time I thought the casual counterpart encompassed all activity that could not be described as serious. How shortsighted that observation was will become evident in the next section on project-based leisure.

Casual leisure is considerably less substantial than serious leisure and offers no career of the sort found in the latter. Its types – there are eight (see Figure 2.1) – include

- *play* (e.g., daydreaming, dabbling at an activity, fiddling with something);
- *relaxation* (e.g., idling, napping, strolling, sitting, lounging, sun tanning);
- *passive entertainment* (e.g., popular TV, pleasurable reading, mass market recorded music);
- *active entertainment* (e.g., games of chance, party games);
- *sociable conversation* (e.g., gossiping, joking, talking about the weather);
- *sensory stimulation* (e.g., sex, eating, drinking alcohol, sightseeing);
- *casual volunteering* (as opposed to serious leisure, or career, volunteering; casual volunteering includes handing out leaflets, stuffing envelopes, and collecting money door-to-door);
- *pleasurable aerobic activity* (discussed as follows).

The last and newest type of casual leisure to be identified – pleasurable aerobic activity – refers to physical activities requiring effort sufficient to cause marked increase in respiration and heart rate (Stebbins, 2004d). As applied here, the term 'aerobic activity' is broad in scope. It encompasses all activity that calls for such effort. This, to be sure, includes the routines pursued collectively in (narrowly conceived of) aerobics classes and those pursued individually by way of televised or video-taped programs of aerobics. Yet, as with its passive and active cousins in entertainment, pleasurable aerobic activity is basically casual leisure. That is, to do such activity requires little more than minimal skill, knowledge, or experience. Examples include the game of the Hash House Harriers (a type of treasure hunt in the outdoors, see the home page at http://www.gthhh.com), kickball (a cross between soccer and baseball) (*The Economist*, 2005), 'exergames' for children (a video game played on a dance floor) (Gerson, 2010), and children's pastimes such as hide-and-seek.

Note that people may dabble (as play) in the same kinds of activities pursued seriously by amateurs, hobbyists, and career volunteers. Being unaware of this difference, some writers have labeled as 'amateurish' all amateur activity, an assessment that the foregoing pages show is ill-founded (e.g., *The Cult of the Amateur* by Andrew Keen, 2007).

People seem to pursue the different types of casual leisure in combinations of two and three at least as often as they pursue them separately. For instance, every type can be relaxing, producing in this fashion play-relaxation, passive entertainment-relaxation, and so on. Various combinations of play and sensory stimulation are also possible, as in experimenting, in deviant or non-deviant ways, with drug use, sexual activity, and thrill seeking through movement. Additionally, sociable conversation accompanies some sessions of sensory stimulation (e.g., recreational drug use, curiosity seeking, displays of beauty) as well as some sessions of relaxation and active and passive entertainment. Though in the latter two, such conversation normally tends to be rather truncated.

This brief review of the types of casual leisure brings out in detail the essential hedonism motivating this type of leisure. All produce a significant level of pure pleasure, or enjoyment, for their modern-day sybarites. In broad, colloquial language, 'casual leisure' could serve as the scientific term for the practice of doing what comes naturally. Yet, paradoxically, this leisure is by no means wholly frivolous, for we shall see shortly that some clear and substantial benefits come from pursuing it. Moreover, unlike the evanescent hedonic property of casual leisure itself, its benefits are enduring.

It follows that terms like 'pleasure' and 'enjoyment' are the more appropriate descriptors of the rewards of casual leisure. These two stand in contrast to 'fulfillment' and 'rewardingness', which best describe the rewards gained in serious leisure. At least, the serious leisure participants that I have interviewed over the years were inclined to describe their involvements as fulfilling or rewarding rather than pleasurable or enjoyable. Still, overlap exists, for both casual and serious leisure offer the hedonic reward of self-gratification (see reward number 5). Sometimes a serious activity is also 'fun' to do, though rarely is its fun aspect the main reason for doing it, which is the motive for much of casual leisure.

Benefits of casual leisure

Notwithstanding its hedonic nature, casual leisure is by no means wholly inconsequential, for some clear costs and benefits accrue from pursuing it. Moreover, in contrast to the evanescent hedonic property of casual leisure itself, these costs and benefits are enduring. We have so far been able to identify six benefits, or outcomes, of casual leisure. But since this is a preliminary list – my first attempt at developing one – it is certainly possible that future research and theorizing could add to it (Stebbins, 2007b, pp. 41–43).

One lasting benefit of casual leisure is the creativity and discovery it sometimes engenders. Serendipity is 'the quintessential form of informal experimentation, accidental discovery, and spontaneous invention' (Stebbins, 2001a). It usually underlies these two processes, suggesting that serendipity and casual leisure are at times closely aligned. In casual leisure, as elsewhere, serendipity can lead to highly varied results. These include a new understanding of a home gadget or government policy, a sudden realization that a particular plant or bird exists in the neighborhood, or a different way of making artistic sounds on a musical instrument. Such creativity or discovery is unintended, however, and is therefore accidental. Moreover, in casual leisure it is not ordinarily the result of an interest in trying to solve a problem, since most of the time people enjoying this kind of activity are not motivated thus. Usually, problems for which solutions must be found emerge at work, while meeting non-work obligations, or during serious leisure. Yet, serendipity might result from dabbling, possibly influencing the decision to start a fulfillment career.

Another benefit springs from what has come to be known as *edutainment*, a portmanteau word coined in 1975 by Christopher Daniels (*New World Encyclopedia*, 2008). His term joins 'education' and 'entertainment' in reference to another benefit of casual leisure, one that comes with participating in such mass entertainment as watching films and television programs, listening to popular music, and reading popular books and articles. Theme parks and museums are also considered sources of edutainment. While consuming media or frequenting places of this sort, these participants inadvertently learn something of substance about the social and physical world in which they live. They are, in a word, entertained and educated in the same breath. Pleasurable historical novels provide some edutainment for the reading set.

Third, casual leisure affords regeneration, or re-creation, possibly even more so than its counterpart, serious leisure, since the latter can sometimes be intense. Of course, many a leisure studies specialist has observed that leisure in general affords relaxation or entertainment, if not both, and that these constitute two of its principal benefits. What is new, then, in the observation just made is that it distinguishes between casual and serious leisure. And more importantly the emphasis is placed on the enduring effects of relaxation and entertainment when they help enhance overall equanimity, doing so most notably in the interstices between periods of intense activity (Kleiber, 2000).

Still, apropos relaxation it is sometimes difficult to separate casual and serious leisure. Consider as an example the personal use of such systems as yoga and tai-chi. Among their principal goals are enabling and encouraging participants to meditate. One by-product of such meditation is relaxation. But first the novice must learn the various moves and positions as well as the philosophy behind them. This indicates that these systems, even though their goal is relaxation, are complex enough to be considered hobbies. They are therefore serious leisure.

A fourth benefit that may flow from participation in casual leisure originates in the development and maintenance of interpersonal relationships. One of its types, the sociable conversation, is particularly fecund in this regard. But other types when shared, as sometimes happens during sensory stimulation and passive and active entertainment, can also have the same effect. The interpersonal relationships in question are many and varied. They include those that form between friends, spouses, and members of families. Such relationships can foster personal psychological growth by promoting new shared interests. And during this process, new positive appraisals of oneself may become possible (Hutchinson & Kleiber, 2005).

Furthermore, some forms of casual and serious leisure offer the reward of *social attraction*, or the appeal of being with other people while participating in a common activity. Nevertheless, even though some casual and serious leisure participants share certain rewards, further research on this question will likely show that these two types experience them in sharply different ways. For instance, consider the social attraction of belonging to a barbershop chorus or a company of actors. Their members engage in a great deal of specialized shoptalk, which they dearly like. Such talk differs dramatically from that of a group of people playing a party game or enjoying a boat tour. Shoptalk is highly unlikely to occur in these latter gatherings.

Well-being is still another benefit that can flow from participating in casual leisure. Speaking only for the realm of leisure, perhaps the greatest sense of well-being is achieved when a person develops an *optimal leisure lifestyle*. Such a lifestyle is 'the deeply satisfying pursuit during free time of one or more substantial, absorbing forms of serious leisure, complemented by a judicious amount of casual leisure' (Stebbins, 2007b). People find optimal leisure lifestyles by partaking of leisure activities that individually, and also in combination, realize human potential and enhance quality of life and well-being. Project-based leisure, to be discussed shortly, can also enhance a person's leisure lifestyle. The previously mentioned study of kayakers, snowboarders, and mountain and ice climbers revealed that the vast majority of the three samples used various forms of casual leisure to optimally round out their use of free time. For them, their serious leisure was a central life interest. Nonetheless, their casual leisure contributed to their overall well-being. It allowed for relaxation, regeneration, sociability, entertainment, and other activities less intense than their serious leisure.

Still, well-being experienced during free time is more than this. For this kind of leisure, say Hutchinson and Kleiber (2005), can contribute to self-protection, as by buffering stress and sustaining coping efforts. Casual leisure can also preserve or restore a sense of self. This was sometimes achieved in their samples when their respondents rediscovered in casual leisure fundamental personal or familial values or a view of themselves as caring people.

Costs

As with serious leisure the casual type has its costs, albeit with one exception, not always the same ones. Some arise because the potential benefits of casual leisure have not been realized. We have so far been able to confirm five costs.

One is boredom, an unmistakable sign of momentary absence of well-being, or momentary presence of low quality of life. Boredom seems most likely to appear when the participant experiences none of the aforementioned benefits and therefore becomes disinterested in both amount and kind of casual leisure at the moment. Weariness and restlessness are bound to follow. Still, boredom is no ineluctable feature of casual leisure, as its place in an optimal leisure lifestyle clearly attests. Rather, it is a possible situational condition lurking in the background, ready to spring out and spoil the person's fun should the latter somehow lose appeal.

Second, casual leisure is, in most instances, unlikely to produce for its enthusiasts a distinctive leisure identity. Few people are inclined to proclaim to the world that they are, for example, inveterate nappers, television watchers, or consumers of fast food. To the extent that faceless causal leisure dominates the free time of people, this less than optimal balance of leisure activities deprives them of one or more leisure identities that they could otherwise have. For instance, Ken Roberts (1999, pp. 9–13), after analyzing the literature in the area concluded, notwithstanding arguments to the contrary, that today's evanescent youth scenes fail to offer special identities to those who frequent them. Leisure of the kind found in these scenes can enhance fleeting self-confidence and help foster momentary positive self-images, but it is too superficial and transient to generate a special identity.

This situation also suggests a third cost: large blocks of casual leisure, even if not boring, leave little time for serious leisure and therefore in yet another way deprive the person of an optimal leisure lifestyle. Also at issue here is a significant reduction, or at least significant barrier to the rise, in well-being and quality of life. Exclusive or nearly exclusive pursuit of pure pleasure, or hedonism, may bring a certain level of happiness, but it can never bring the richest expression of that emotion. German philosopher Arthur Schopenhauer commented on at least two occasions about happiness, boredom, and casual leisure. On one of them he observed that 'the most general survey shows us that the two foes of human happiness are pain and boredom' (from *Essays. Personality, or What a Man Is*). Later, he noted that 'there is no more mistaken path to happiness than worldliness, revelry, high life' (from *Our Relations with Ourselves*).

A fourth cost of casual leisure is that, most often, it makes only a limited contribution to self and community. Unless the person has created, discovered, or learned something new, casual leisure is unlikely to produce a distinctive identity, which constitutes one aspect of this cost. Others aspects include the common failure of casual leisure to generate good feelings about oneself – the value of self-esteem – and to lead to self-development – the value of personal improvement. Further, much of casual leisure, outside its often times considerable economic punch, otherwise contributes lit-tle to the development of the community. Development in this sense means participation by community members in an activity result-ing in improvement of one or more of its identifiable aspects and strengthening communal patterns of human and institutional inter-relationships (Ploch, 1976, p. 8; Pedlar, 1996). Of note, however, are casual leisure volunteers; they are exceptions to the observations just made. Their work does contribute to self and community (Stebbins, 1996).

The fifth cost, one shared with the serious pursuits, are the occa-sional disappointments encountered in some casual activities. How often have we gone to the cinema or a music performance and left, perhaps before it ended, deeply disappointed? Or the scenery we paid a fancy price to see cannot be viewed because of inclement weather. Or the lively conversation we hoped to have with colleagues after work turns into a bitching session about a superior whom you like. We expect disappointments in life, but just the same they tarnish a bit its rewards and benefits. Even hedonic casual leisure is not immune from such unpleasantness.

Project-based leisure

Project-based leisure is the third type of leisure activity and the one most recently to join the other two (Stebbins, 2005b). It is a short-term, reasonably complicated, one-off or occasional, though infrequent, creative undertaking carried out in free time, or time free of disagreeable obligation. Such leisure requires considerable plan-ning, effort, and sometimes skill or knowledge. Yet it is neither serious leisure nor intended to develop into such. The adjective 'occasional' describes widely spaced undertakings for such regular occasions as religious festivals, someone's birthday, or a national holiday. Volun-teering for a sports event may be seen as an occasional project. The adjective 'creative' stresses that the undertaking results in something new or different, by showing imagination and perhaps routine skill or knowledge. Though most projects would appear to be continu-ously pursued until completed, it is conceivable that some might be interrupted for several weeks, months, and even years. For example, a stone wall in the back garden that gets finished only after its builder recovers from an operation on his strained back. Only a rudimentary social world springs up around the typical project. Nonetheless, it does in its own way and bring together friends, neighbors, or relatives (e.g., through a genealogical project or Christmas celebration). Or it may draw the individual participant into an organizational setting, as happens when volunteering for a sports event or major convention.

Moreover, it appears that in some instances project-based leisure springs from a sense of obligation to undertake it. If so, it is nonetheless done as leisure, as uncoerced activity, in the sense that the obligation is in fact 'agreeable' – the project creator in executing the project anticipates finding fulfillment, obligated or not. And worth exploring, given that some obligations can be pleasant and attractive, is the nature and extent of leisure-like projects carried out as part of paid employment. Furthermore, this discussion jibes with the additional criterion that the project, to qualify as project-based leisure, must be *seen by the project creator* as fundamentally uncoerced, fulfilling activity. Finally, note that project-based leisure cannot, by definition, refer to projects executed as part of a person's serious leisure. Examples include mounting a star night as an amateur astronomer or displaying a model train as a collector.

Though not serious leisure, project-based leisure is similar enough to it to justify using the SLP to develop a parallel framework for exploring this class of activities. A primary difference is that project-based leisure fails to imbue participants with a sense of career. Otherwise, however, there is need here to persevere, acquire in some cases certain skills or knowledge, and, invariably, put out some effort. Also present are recognizable benefits, a special identity, and often a social world of sorts. Although the latter, as it appears, is usually less complicated than those in which most serious leisure activities are framed. And it may happen at times that, even when not intended at the moment as participation in a type of serious leisure, the skilled, artistic, or intellectual aspects of the project prove highly attractive. Realizing this, the participant decides after the fact to make a leisure career of the activity as a hobbyist or amateur pursuit.

Project-based leisure is also capable of generating many of the rewards experienced in serious leisure. And, as in serious leisure so in project-based leisure: these rewards constitute part of the motivational basis for engaging in such highly fulfilling activity. Furthermore, motivation to undertake a leisure project may have an organizational base, much as many other forms of leisure do

(Stebbins, 2002). My observations suggest that small groups, grass-roots associations (volunteer groups with few or no paid staff), and volunteer organizations (paid-staff groups using volunteer help) are the most common types of organizations in which people undertake project-based leisure.

Motivationally speaking, project-based leisure may be attractive in substantial part because it, unlike serious leisure, rarely demands long-term commitment. Even occasional projects carry with them the sense that the undertaking in question has a definite end. Indeed, it may even be terminated prematurely. Thus project-based leisure is not what Robert Dubin (1992) called a 'central life interest'. Rather, it is viewed by participants as fulfilling (as distinguished from enjoyable or hedonic) activity that can be experienced comparatively quickly, though certainly not as quickly as casual leisure.

Project-based leisure fits into leisure lifestyle in its own peculiar way as interstitial activity. In this, it resembles some casual leisure but not most serious leisure. Project-based leisure can therefore help shape a person's optimal leisure lifestyle. For instance, it can often be pursued at times convenient for the participant. It follows that project-based leisure is nicely suited to people who, out of proclivity or extensive non-leisure obligations or both, reject serious leisure and, yet, who also have no appetite for a steady diet of casual leisure. Among the candidates for project-based leisure are people with heavy workloads; homemakers, mothers, and fathers with extensive domestic responsibilities; unemployed individuals who, though looking for work, still have time at the moment for (I suspect, mostly one-shot) projects; and avid serious leisure enthusiasts who want a temporary change in their leisure lifestyle. Retired people who often do have time for discretionary activity may find project-based leisure attractive as a way of adding spice and variety to their lifestyles. Beyond these special categories of participant, project-based leisure offers a form of substantial leisure to all adults, adolescents, and even children looking for something interesting and exciting to do in free time that is neither casual nor serious leisure.

Types of project-based leisure

It was noted in the definition just presented that project-based leisure is not all the same. Whereas systematic exploration may reveal others, two types are evident at this time: one-shot projects and occasional projects. These are presented next using the classificatory framework for amateur, hobbyist, and volunteer activities developed earlier in this chapter.

One-shot projects

In all these projects people generally use the talents and knowledge they have at hand, even though for some projects they may seek certain instructions beforehand, including reading a book or taking a short course. And some projects resembling hobbyist activity participation may require a modicum of preliminary conditioning. Always, the goal is to undertake successfully the one-off project and nothing more, and sometimes a small amount of background preparation is necessary for this. It is possible that a survey would show that most project-based leisure is hobbyist in character and the next most common, a kind of volunteering. First, the following hobbyist-like projects have so far been identified, with those in the areas of making and tinkering, the liberal arts, and the arts projects often requiring some background utilitarian reading:

Making and tinkering:

- Interlacing, interlocking, and knot-making from kits
- Other kit assembly projects (e.g., stereo tuner, craft store projects)
- Do-it-yourself projects done primarily for fulfillment, some of which may even be undertaken with minimal skill and knowledge (e.g., build a rock wall or a fence, finish a room in the basement, plant a special garden); this could turn into an irregular series of such projects, spread over many years, possibly even transforming the participant into a hobbyist

Liberal arts:

- Family history (not as ongoing hobby): genealogy, scrapbooking, memory journaling
- Tourism: special trip, not as part of an extensive personal tour program, to visit different parts of a region, a continent, or much of the world
- Renaissance-man reading projects (e.g., read all the Pulitzer Prize winners in letters and drama for a particular year or set of years)

Activity participation: long backpacking trip, canoe trip; one-off mountain ascent (e.g., Fuji, Rainier, Kilimanjaro).

One-off volunteering projects are also common, though possibly somewhat less so than hobbyist-like projects. And less common than either are the amateur-like projects, which seem to concentrate in the sphere of theater.

Volunteering (see Table 1.1):

- Volunteer at a convention or conference, whether local, national, or international in scope
- Volunteer at a sporting competition, whether local, national, or international in scope
- Volunteer at an arts festival or special exhibition mounted in a museum
- Volunteer to help restore human life or wildlife after a natural or human-made disaster caused by, for instance, a hurricane, earthquake, oil spill, or industrial accident

Arts projects:

- Entertainment theater: produce a skit or one-off community pageant; prepare a home film, video, or set of photos
- Public speaking: prepare a talk for a reunion, an after-dinner speech, an oral position statement on an issue to be discussed at a community meeting
- Memoirs: therapeutic audio, visual, and written productions by the elderly; life histories and autobiographies (all ages); accounts of personal events (all ages)

Occasional projects

The occasional projects seem more likely to originate in or be motivated by agreeable obligation than their one-off cousins. Examples of occasional projects include the sum of the culinary, decorative, or other creative activities undertaken, for example, at home or at work for a religious occasion or someone's birthday. Likewise, national holidays and similar celebrations sometimes inspire individuals to mount occasional projects consisting of an ensemble of inventive elements.

Unlike one-off projects occasional projects have the potential to become routinized, which happens when new creative possibilities no longer come to mind as the participant arrives at a fulfilling formula wanting no further modification. North Americans who decorate their homes the same way each Christmas season exemplify this situation. Indeed, it can happen that, over the years, such projects may lose their appeal, but not their necessity. Thus they turn into disagreeable obligations, with their authors no longer defining them as leisure.

And, lest it be overlooked, note that one-off projects also hold the possibility of becoming unpleasant. Thus, the hobbyist genealogist gets overwhelmed with the details of family history and the challenge of verifying dates. The thought of putting in time and effort doing something once considered leisure but which she now dislikes makes no sense. Likewise, volunteering for a project may turn sour. The volunteer is now faced with a disagreeable obligation, which however, must still be honored. This is leisure no more.

Conclusions

My aim in this chapter has been to paint a broad portrait of today's leisure activities and, in this way, move well beyond their image in the popular mind as being wholly casual. In discussing the fulfillment careers, it is critical to know which kinds of leisure (and work) lend themselves to this kind of passage through life and which do not. Still, the leisure domain is complex, for – as noted earlier – casual and project-based leisure do sometimes figure in the initial steps of a fulfillment career in a serious pursuit. A key advantage of the SLP is that it keeps such complexity at center stage. There it sensitizes us to the many features of work and leisure and, in this instance, how they bear on fulfillment careers.

With this conceptual background in mind, we turn now to how people start those careers.

2
Starting a Fulfillment Career

Fulfillment careers are born in particular activities enjoyed in daily life, where from time to time, people explore the vast world of free-time interests. Typically, these beginnings are prosaic, especially compared with the participant's career when fulfillment is at its apogee. This is not to say that such careers inevitably reach the heights of those enjoyed by the best movie stars, sports heroes, successful small business people, or respected trades-workers. Nevertheless, no one seeking a fulfillment career *starts* out at the top.

The purpose of this chapter is to examine the key processes and conditions that facilitate embarking on a fulfillment career. One of them is accidental discovery, discussed here as dabbling. Another is memorable contact with an exemplar of the work/leisure activity on which such a career is founded. Both processes may inspire some strategic planning, arranging for deeper learning, and parallel participation as a neophyte.

Dabbling

So far as the study of leisure is concerned, 'dabbler' first appeared as a scientific concept in 1979 (Stebbins, 1979, pp. 20, 30). Then, as now, dabbling has been conceived of as a kind of play, which starting with my conceptualization, was classified as one type of casual leisure (Stebbins, 1982; 1997). The amateur–professional–public system of relationships, introduced in my 1979 book, placed the dabbler as part of the public of the other two, as someone who is from time to time amused while trying to emulate performance of a given art, sport, or entertainment activity. But in a real performance it is not, for by definition the dabbler lacks the training and practice needed for this.

This view of the dabbler – as part of a public – has tended to obscure this leisure participant's broader relationship with the amateurs and professionals. Fortunately, development of the SLP has given us in a more encompassing theoretic orientation. It encourages and facilitates seeing in as rich detail as possible the many ways in which dabblers, amateurs, hobbyists, professionals, and, most recently, project-based leisure enthusiasts are related.

The proposition that dabbling is the first step taken by some great professionals in launching their careers may seem preposterous. It can be hard to imagine an accomplished pianist having once hesitantly tapped out notes on a keyboard or a famous soccer player having once clumsily kicked a ball around a local park. By no means all professional careers originate in this kind of play, but for those that do with disinterestedness is, ironically, the attitude that precedes deep commitment to the serious pursuit.

As just noted dabbling is a kind of play. More particularly, it is spontaneous activity engaged in for its own sake, for curiosity and hedonic experience. It is 'disinterested' in the sense that no long-term goal is envisioned while dabbling; the participant simply wants certain immediate experiences.[1] Furthermore, these experiences need not be physical, as they usually are, for example, in music and certain outdoor activities, but may be mental such as in flights of imagination triggered through reading (Stebbins, 2013b).

Components of dabbling

Dabbling has at least three components: sensory, social, and accessibility. The sensory component is psychological – the sensations generated through one or more of the senses. It is experienced while doing the core activities of dabbling. They are what we most commonly associate with dabbling: engaging in such activities with the intention of satisfying curiosity and experiencing agreeable sensations. In music, dabblers may experience percussion, melody, pitch, or, more rarely it appears, harmony or rhythm. Combinations of these are possible, as well. In painting, dabblers play visually with different colored oils or, more probably given their cost, different water colors. Touch and sight are experienced when, in basketball, one playfully bounces and attempts to put the ball in the basket. Are not some people (nonoenophiles) at wine tastings dabbling with taste and smell?

The other two components are contextual. Turning to the social component it appears that most dabbling is mimetic. In music, the dabbler has seen or heard, if not both, someone else either dabble with or play more or less properly an instrument. Or that person might be dabbling at singing a melody. Likewise, dabblers in painting and basketball may well be mimicking other dabblers or serious participants in the same activity. The dabbler in wine tasting, however, is probably not copying someone else, though this person may have been instructed on what to look for and how to savor the wine most effectively.

The family, nuclear and extended, is a main arena for childhood dabbling, exemplified in the boy or girl who watches, for example, a sibling, parent, aunt, cousin, or grandparent play or dabble on a guitar or canvas, play a sport, or engage in a hobby (e.g., cooking, yoga, reading). The parents of Anthony Tommasini (2013), music critic and recording pianist, bought him early in his life a small toy piano, on which he happily picked out tunes. This was his 'eureka moment'. Children might also try to imitate any of these people as they sing or hum. Furthermore, mimetic exemplars are also in abundance today on television, DVDs, Web sites, and onstage. How many adolescent guitar players got their start mimicking someone they saw on TV, doing so on an instrument laying around home or received as a gift from a family member?

This brings us to the accessibility component. Would-be dabblers must have something to fiddle with (except, of course, vocal dabblers). What if there was no guitar at home and no one was willing or able to buy one? What if the object of the would-be dabbler's musical affection is only available in certain locations, as would be true for a harp, tympani, or pipe organ? Again, a child could get the urge to dabble on one of these, having seen and heard it played at a church service or symphony orchestra concert. But getting access to the instrument merely for hedonic pleasure is improbable. Would-be dabblers in ice hockey living in hot climates, in star-gazing living in light-polluted cities, and in hunting living far from huntable wildlife face similar problems of access to key resources.

In short, fulfillment careers, to the extent that they root in dabbling, get off to a chancy start.

Dabbling and the CL–SL continuum

Nonetheless, some people do dabble at an activity, and a proportion of this group moves on to pursuing it more seriously as a neophyte. Yet, dabbling is impossible in certain activities, forcing would-be enthusiasts to start as neophytes. Here, to learn of their affinity for it, they must actually undertake some careful preparation. Whether people embark on their fulfillment careers indirectly as dabblers or directly as neophytes, they do so within a serious pursuit. Scientific discussion of this transition has come to be known as the 'CL–SL [casual–serious leisure] Continuum'. A central question here has revolved around whether casual leisure dabbling is a precursor to becoming a neophyte in a serious pursuit. The preceding observations suggest that this happens adventitiously, only in certain kinds of activities, and only for participants who want to get serious about their leisure.

Thus fulfillment careers begin with becoming a neophyte in that pursuit (Stebbins, 2007b). Being a neophyte means, among other things, signaling to self, and often, certain other people the intention to get better at it. This is achieved along the lines of four fundamental dimensions: effort, skill, knowledge, and experience. Gains along these four, as they apply to the activity in question, put the participant on the road to personal development, self-fulfillment, and a career in the activity. Neophytes manifest their intention to get better by engaging in such formative activities as taking lessons, reading extensively, practicing fundamental skills, observing experienced participants, and the like.

Neophytes are not casual leisure participants. Even the erstwhile dabblers have moved away from their hedonic interest in the activity. Still, the fact that some neophytes have been attracted earlier to the activity purely for its raw enjoyment is not to be ignored. Examples include the child who taps out chop sticks and other ditties on the piano and later becomes interested in piano lessons; the back garden star gazer using a cheap telescope who decides to get more serious by joining the local astronomy club; the joke-telling life of the party who, wanting to become a stand-up comic, mounts an 'open-mic' stage, and with that launches a career in the art. The fulfillment career begins with a neophyte level of interest in the activity, but the casual dabbling as these examples show can be a crucial precursor. If priming the pump is what makes the pump work, then the priming cannot be dismissed as a minor step in the process.

The seriousness dimension of involvement

Dabblers have been the last in this group of concepts to be systematically integrated into the SLP (Stebbins, 2012b). That is, what has become known as the 'seriousness dimension' has only recently attracted some significant scholarly attention. Shen and Yarnal (2010), Derom and Taks (2011), and Scott (2012), have elaborated in the greatest detail yet the idea of the CL–SL continuum. These authors have also demonstrated such variation in sport and hobbies. They have added needed empirical precision to the nominal scale of intensity of involvement in an SL activity.

This involvement scale was introduced over 20 years ago (Stebbins, 1992, pp. 46–48). There I observed that, at any point in time, serious leisure enthusiasts may be classified as either *devotees* or *participants*. The devotees are highly dedicated to their pursuits, whereas the participants are only moderately interested in it, albeit significantly more so than dabblers. Participants typically greatly outnumber devotees. Along this dimension, devotees and participants are operationally differentiated primarily by the different amounts of time they commit to their serious leisure, as manifested in engaging in the core activity, training or preparing for it, reading about it, and similar indicators.

This is, however, a rather crude scale of intensity of involvement in a serious leisure activity, a weakness not missed by Siegenthaler and O'Dell (2003). Their findings from a study of older golfers and successful aging revealed that data on leisure career are more effectively considered according to three types, labeled by them as 'social', 'moderate', and 'core devotee'. The moderate is equivalent to the participant, whereas the social player falls into a class of players who are more skilled and involved than dabblers but less skilled and involved than the moderates (participants). To keep terminology consistent with past theory and research and the generality of the earlier two terms, I have suggested that we calibrate this new, more detailed, involvement scale with appropriate new terms: *participant*, *moderate devotee*, and *core devotee* (Stebbins, 2007b, p. 21). Moreover, the scale should include neophytes and, as precursors, dabblers and participants in project-based leisure. This expanded SLP involvement scale is presented in Figure 2.1.

Considering this involvement scale and the CL–SL continuum together has a number of advantages. For instance, they bring casual leisure and dabbling to the fore by also focusing attention on the process of either deciding to become or drifting toward becoming a neophyte in a serious leisure activity. More particularly, the continuum now gives full recognition to casual and project-based leisure as *possible* preliminary steps in the process of choosing and pursuing a leisure activity.

We must remember, however, that movement along the CL–SL continuum is by no means inevitable. Thus many a casual leisure activity holds little or no possibility of leading on to a career in serious leisure. Included in this list are relaxation (e.g., napping, strolling in the park), sensory stimulation (e.g., sex, sightseeing, drinking alcohol), and casual volunteering (e.g., handing out leaflets on a street corner, taking tickets for a performance of an amateur play). Furthermore, even with their casual interest in an activity capable of being pursued seriously, some participants never become neophytes. How many people, including children, simply forever dabble at tennis, bird-watching, swimming or playing the piano? Meanwhile, activities exist that are so complex, require so much initial skill and knowledge, that entering them, even to participate minimally, is only possible with significant training and knowledge. Quilters, ski jumpers, sky divers, oboe players, and ballet dancers, for example, have to acquire a rudimentary level of competence before they can begin to do their activity, even at its simplest. They enter the CL–SL continuum as neophytes, bypassing altogether the exploratory delights of casual leisure dabbling.

Recreational specialization

Farther along the CL–SL continuum some participants toy with the possibility of specializing in their serious pursuit. 'Recreational specialization' is both process and product. As a process, it refers to a progressive narrowing of interests within a complex leisure activity: 'a continuum of behavior from the general to the particular', as Hobson Bryan (1977, p. 175) put it. Viewed as an aspect of a serious pursuit, specialization may be seen as part of the leisure career experienced in those complex activities that offer participants who want to focus

Figure 2.1 SLP involvement scale

their interests an opportunity to do so (Stebbins, 2005c). In particular, when specialization occurs, it unfolds as a process within the development or establishment stage, possibly spanning the two, or should the participant change specialties, it unfolds within the maintenance stage.

In career terminology (see later in this chapter), developing a specialty is a career turning point. Bryan's research centered on specialization among trout fishers, some of whom did this by moving from general fly fishing to using only dry flies. David Scott (2012) provides a review of theory and research in this lively area of leisure studies as it relates to the SLP.

Memorable contact

As briefly alluded to in the introduction to this chapter, memorable contact with an exemplar of the work/leisure activity on which a fulfillment career is founded can be another starting point for that career. Here, too, we lack systematic research. Still, anecdotal data do exist, thanks particularly to a series on the catalytic event that vaulted, among others, various actors, dancers, painters, sculptors, and musicians into neophyte status (*New York Times*, 2013a; 2013b; 2013c). Hearing a certain musical performance, viewing a certain painting or sculpture, watching a certain dancer or actor provided the impetus that propelled the observer into the art as, initially, an amateur.

If casual leisure is a precursor of such memorable contact, it is that participants come to their catalytic events in search of, for example, entertainment or sensory stimulation. As with dabbling this search usually is an adventitious occurrence and, it follows, their fulfillment careers here are also off to a chancy start. Nonetheless, once focused on the activity as a neophyte, these participants also begin to move at their own pace along the involvement scale. How far they go depends on a multitude of factors (see chapters 3–7).

Loving the core activities

Amateurs, hobbyists, and career volunteers are all in the deepest sense of the word *amators* of the core activities that constitute the very essence of their passion.[2] Thus, artists love creating their canvases, poker players love playing poker, calligraphers love making letters with their pens, and volunteer docents at the zoo love teaching about particular animals. A key question that any examination of fulfillment careers must ask is why do serious participants fall in love with their core activities? Why do they become *amators*? For without this love (or passion), it may be argued that serious pursuit of those activities will fail to develop. Generally put, what is it about the core activities of a serious pursuit that has magnetic appeal for some people while repelling others or at least failing to ignite any solid interest from them?

At present, this area is the Achilles heel of the study of fulfillment careers. Why, because research on it is sparse. Sinha (1979) found that the core activity of shaping a pot from a lump of clay turning on a wheel was regarded by her respondents as meditative and soothing. Birders have been shown to be motivated by a fascination for birds, astronomers by the wonder of the heavens, and archaeologists by an abiding curiosity about a bygone, usually local, civilization (Stebbins, 1979, p. 170; 1980, p. 43; Kellert, 1985). But none of these studies examined in detail the love for the core activity.[3]

Still, we may say at this early stage of conceptual development that love of a serious leisure activity is comprised of at least two conditions: taste and talent. Having a taste, or predilection, for an activity refers to how attractive the thought is of doing it. Thus, some people thrill at the possibility of playing the guitar, cooking gourmet dinners, or volunteering with the local police service. Others find little appeal in such activities, but vibrate instead on raising horses, collecting coins, or serving on ski patrol.

Talent and taste for an activity seem most of the time to go together. Yet, this happy combination is not inevitable, since a participant may discover earlier or later that the hoped-for talent is not there at the level needed to generate fulfillment. Talent, in particular, may become an issue far into a fulfillment career, as the participant discovers at an advanced level of the core activity – commonly in late development – that he or she lacks the ability to succeed in it. Examples include insufficient finger dexterity on the piano, weak sense of balance in dance, incapacity to see the big picture required of an effective president of the board.

Other than these observations, we are left to speculate about this love for the core activity, much as I just did for artists, poker players, calligraphers, and docents. Even then I sketched a shallow picture of that sentiment. Better are the first-hand personal accounts reported in autobiographies or broadcast on the Internet, which speak to, for example, 'why I like to write' and 'why I like to paint'.[4] Such an account can contain informative detail about the author's love for the core activity and its place in that person's life, suggesting thereby that this sentiment is often, perhaps always, many-faceted and deeply nuanced. But studying this area using the Internet meets with sampling problems, in that such accounts remain to be written for most of the serious pursuits (as listed in Figure 1.1).

Given the paucity of research on the nature of the love of core activities, I can do little more in this book than highlight a pressing need to close this gap. Speculation and even the Internet accounts are inadequate substitutes for carefully collected data on this crucial element of the fulfillment career. My plan in this book, then, is to say little more about the matter, with the hope that what I have just said will spark an interest in studying the love for core activities as an incentive to begin and continue with a fulfillment career.

The leisure career

With experience and determination the neophyte amateur, hobbyist, or volunteer advances according to amount of effort, talent, determination, and the like toward the statuses of participant, moderate devotee, or core devotee – and possibly on to devotee work. In music after neophyte, these next three levels are occupied by more accomplished amateurs. Stebbins (1978), Booth (1999), and Regelski (2007), for example, have described for classical music many of the distinctive characteristics of these levels, including especially the artistic excellence of its moderate and core devotees. Puddephatt (2005) examined these levels as they are experienced by committed amateurs in chess. Stebbins (2005a) studied such development in the hobbies of kayaking, snowboarding, and mountain climbing, around the same time that Heuser (2005) undertook similar research in lawn bowls.

Subjectively speaking, participants experience this stream of personal development as a 'leisure career'. The term suggests that it should apply only to status passage within activities engaged in during free time outside of work. But, with publication of the statement on the definition of leisure, devotee work, now conceived of as essentially serious leisure, has become an integral part of the leisure career framework (Stebbins, 2012a). In other words, these careers are experienced in the serious pursuits, where some participants go so far as to wind up making a living in what was earlier a purely amateur, hobbyist, or career volunteer activity. Indeed, a leisure career may, as we shall see, even culminate in retirement from a work role, that is, if these retirees do not return to their serious leisure roots (e.g., the retired professional hockey player who subsequently plays in an adult recreational league).

It was stated in the preceding chapter that serious leisure is the systematic pursuit of an amateur, hobbyist, or volunteer activity that participants find so substantial and interesting that, in the typical case, they launch themselves on a career centered on acquiring and expressing its special skills, knowledge, and experience. Yet, there exists in common sense the widespread tendency to see the idea of career as applying only to occupations. Here, I use the term much more broadly, however, doing so in harmony with Goffman's (1961) elaboration of the idea of 'moral career'. Broadly conceived of, careers are possible in all substantial, complicated roles and activities, including especially those in work, leisure, deviance, politics, religion, and interpersonal relationships.[5]

A second quality is, as indicated earlier, that of finding a career in the endeavor, shaped as this career is by its own special contingencies, turning points and stages of achievement and involvement. Exploratory research on careers in serious leisure has so far proceeded from a broad, rather loose definition: a leisure career is the typical course, or passage, of a type of amateur, hobbyist, or volunteer that carries the person from the stage of neophyte into and through a leisure role and possibly into and through a work role.

At each stage in their career history, participants may encounter special contingencies. A *career contingency* is an unintended event, process, or situation that occurs by chance; that is, it lies substantially beyond the control of the people pursuing the career. Career contingencies emanate from changes in leisure or work environments or personal circumstances, or both. Thus the movement of people, whether progressive or retrogressive, through careers is affected by the contingencies they meet along the way. Note, too, that contingencies may be positive or negative. The next chapter contains a discussion of the negative kind.

The idea of a subjective career refers to the participant's recognition and interpretation of the events – past, present, and future – associated with this person's work or leisure activity (Hughes, 1937; Stebbins, 1970). Especially important in any analysis of the subjective side of a career is the participant's interpretation of the turning points expected or already encountered. It is from a description of their subjective careers that we learn how amateurs and professionals have determined continuity in their work and leisure lives – how they see themselves as progressing or declining.

A *turning point* is a juncture at which the nature or direction of an amateur-professional career is seen by the practitioners as having changed significantly. In general, the turning points in a career are the critical events and decisions experienced and made in the course of the work or leisure. Certain career contingencies may be interpreted as turning points; for example, getting injured in a game or discovering a comet. Other important events such as winning an award, succeeding at an audition, and deciding on a specialty, while not contingent, are still seen as turning points. They fail to qualify as contingencies because, to a significant degree, they are caused and controlled by the participants themselves. Some turning points, then, are contingent whereas some are not. Moreover, some are positive and some are not. The career stage most likely to produce turning points is that of establishment.

The essence of any career, whether in work, leisure, or elsewhere, lies in the temporal continuity of the activities associated with it. That is, every serious leisure career both frames and is framed by the never-ending search for certain personal and social rewards (listed in Chapter 1). This search can take months, and in some activities years, before the participant consistently finds deep fulfillment in the pursuit.

Career continuity

In particular, we are accustomed to thinking of this continuity as one of accumulating rewards and a measure of prestige or recognition, as progress along these lines from some starting point. Continuity may, however, also include career retrogression. In the worlds of sport and entertainment, for instance, athletes and artists may reach performance peaks early on, after which the prestige and rewards diminish as the limelight shifts to younger, sometimes more capable practitioners. Serious leisure careers have been empirically examined in my own research as well as, for example, in that of Scott and Godbey (1994); Hastings, Kurth, and Schloder (1996); Baldwin and Norris (1999); Bartram (2001); Puddephatt (2005); Tsaur and Liang (2008); Getz and Andersson (2010); McQuarrie and Jackson (1996); and Lewis, Patterson, and Pegg (2013).

Career continuity may also be observed structurally in one of three ways: within, between, or outside organizations. Careers in organizations such as a community orchestra or hobbyist association only rarely involve the challenge of the 'bureaucratic crawl', to use the imagery of C. Wright Mills. In other words, little or no hierarchy exists for them to climb. Nevertheless, the amateur or hobbyist still gains a profound sense of continuity, and hence career, from his or her more or less steady development as a skilled, experienced, and knowledgeable participant in a particular form of serious leisure and from the deepening satisfaction that accompanies this kind of personal growth. Some volunteer careers are intra-organizational as well.

Still, many amateurs and volunteers as well as some hobbyists have careers that bridge two or more organizations. For them, career continuity stems from their growing reputations as skilled, knowledgeable practitioners and, based on this image, from finding increasingly better leisure opportunities available through various outlets (as in different teams, orchestras, organizations, tournaments, exhibitions, journals, conferences, contests, shows, and the like). Meanwhile, still other amateurs and hobbyists who pursue noncollective lines of leisure (e.g., tennis, painting, clowning, golf, entertainment magic) are free of even this marginal affiliation with an organization. The extra-organizational career of the informal volunteer, the forever willing and sometimes highly skilled and knowledgeable helper of friends, relatives, and neighbors is of this third type.

Career stages

The serious leisure participants who stick with their activities eventually pass through four, possibly five career stages: beginning, developmental, establishment, maintenance, and decline. This is a subjective career. Thus the boundaries separating these stages are imprecise, for as the condition of continuity suggests, the participant passes largely imperceptibly from one to the next. The beginning lasts as long as is necessary for interest in the activity to take root. Development begins when the interest has taken root and its pursuit becomes more or less routine and systematic. Serious leisure participants advance to the establishment stage once they have moved beyond the requirement of having to learn the basics of their activity. During the maintenance stage, the leisure career is in full bloom; here participants are now able to enjoy to the utmost the pursuit of it, the uncertainties of getting established having been put behind them, for the most part. Some enthusiasts move into devotee work at some point during establishment, typically carrying on at that level through maintenance. Finally, by no means do all who are in maintenance face decline, but those who do, typically experience it because of deteriorating mental or physical skills. A more detailed description of the career framework and its five stages is available elsewhere (Stebbins, 1992, chapter 5; on hobbies, see Stebbins, 1996).

The neophytes are beginners, a stage characterized by, among other qualities, that of uncertainty. In music, for example, participants struggle with learning the rudiments of playing their chosen instrument, developing an ear and a sense of time, and learning how to read music. For this to occur most effectively, regular practice and lessons are essential. These participants are no longer dabblers, if indeed they ever were. And it is likewise for tyros in a sport, science, field of entertainment, or genre of career volunteering. Nagging uncertainly is one reason why serious leisure is serious.

Technically, one is not even an amateur, hobbyist, or career volunteer in the early days of being a neophyte. That is, a main early career contingency lies in developing a substantial awareness of the pursuit itself. This may happen abruptly or gradually. For many artists, both fine and popular, there is a memorable, abrupt direct contact with their art that launches their career in it. Evidence for this leap in motivation in the arts as well as in astronomy is set out elsewhere (Stebbins, 1992, pp. 71–72).

In contrast, research suggests that athletic careers have a gradual beginning somewhat along the following lines. While playing pickup football, baseball, and other childhood sports, youngsters gain considerable fulfillment from the expression of athletic interests or from the admiration of others, both adults and peers. Moreover, they may be intrigued by the nature of the sport itself. During this early period, they also discover their aptitude for sport. By pitting their skills against their peers, these youngsters learn whether they excel in physical activities.[6]

Indirect contact, through books, magazines, CDs, television, and the Internet appears to be a common precondition when the beginning stage is gradual. This is especially true for taking up a science or an activity resting on linguistic and interpretative skills such as theater, writing, and stand-up comedy. A committed beginning in these areas is normally only possible in adulthood or late adolescence.

Furthermore, gender stereotypes may push would-be participants in certain directions. Thus, Nardi (1988) found that entertainment magic is traditionally seen as the proper undertaking of males, because of the power, control, and competitive manipulation of others believed to be inherent in the art. By contrast, males have to contend with the public view that ballet dancing, and to a lesser degree theater, are only for females (Perreault, 1988; Levy, 1989). The stereotypes of the gender appropriate sports are particularly well known as in, for example, American football for males (requiring strength and speed) and certain gymnastics events for women (requiring poise and rhythmic movement). As well known is the observation that, at least historically, schools tend to foster the view that science, among other areas, is a boys' subject (Salamon & Robinson, 1987). Meanwhile, Stalp (2007, p. 10) reports that quilting is overwhelmingly a female interest.

Development

Development begins when interest in an activity takes root and its pursuit becomes systematic and routine. To be sure, personal improvement in any serious pursuit lasts only as long as the practitioner stays in it. There is an infinite amount to be learned, experienced, or acquired; even those acknowledged to be the best are still developing in this sense. As a career stage, however, development ends, often gradually, when practitioners see themselves as having reached a point at which they can perform their specialty in the field with relative ease, where they no longer see themselves as learners or students. Passage through development to career establishment is achieved by some amateurs and all professionals.

It was in the study of stand-up comics that I finally found a way to conceptualize, in general terms, the process of development in the serious pursuits (Stebbins, 1990). The scheme that emerged there, generalizable to all these pursuits, consists of five patterns of development. In *the sporadic* pattern the practitioner, rather like the dabbler, participates irregularly in the activity. In the *gradual* pattern, involvement becomes more and more frequent until it reaches a certain level of regularity, at which point the practitioner enters the *steady* pattern of development. Some of those in this last pattern face a need from time to time to interrupt their pursuit of the avocation, say, to work or attend school. They have a *broken-steady* pattern of development. Finally, the *delayed-steady* pattern is found among those practitioners who abandon their avocation for several months early in the development stage, but return to steady involvement later on.

The steady pattern was most common in stand-up comedy, where amateurs performed regularly during weekly 'open-mic' nights after their initial appearance onstage, usually during an open-mic session. Sporadic, broken-steady, and delayed-steady patterns were reported by smaller numbers of comics. My studies of football and baseball, in contrast, suggested that sporadic involvement is most prevalent among youth, and that it holds until they join a team or start taking lessons, as in, for example, golf, tennis, or swimming. At this time, they begin to participate steadily.

Careers at the developmental stage in the fine arts generally resemble those in sport at this point. Whether initial contact with an art is abrupt or gradual, early development is likely to be sporadic. Only when the neophyte enters some sort of formal training program does development proceed more steadily. Delayed and broken patterns appear to be less common here than in stand-up comedy or the other entertainment fields that attract mainly adults. For example, art and sport often attract children whose pursuit of the activity is unlikely to be interrupted by a competing interest (unless it is another budding avocation).

The dominant pattern of development in science falls between that found in art and sport and that found in entertainment, at least among adults. Children and adolescents who enter avocational science appear to follow a pattern undertaken by only a minority entering art and sport. Instead of being sporadically involved, they become gradually involved. The gradual introduction of more science in school probably accounts for this pattern, which holds until the teenager joins a science club or selects a particular science as a university major. At that time, pursuit becomes steady.

Still, the nature of some avocational science is such that development reaches a point where it becomes sporadic, or at least seasonal. Unlike much of art, sport, and entertainment, there are few if any physical skills in science that must be acquired and assiduously maintained through practice. Amateurs can observe stars, for example, when the temperature is comfortable; they can also be forced into inactivity because of a week of cloud or haze. Nevertheless, although northern ornithologists, archaeologists, mineralogists, and mycologists must usually wait for spring to resume pursuit of their avocations, some will still choose to collect data intermittently rather than steadily (on mycologists, see Fine, 1998). And this orientation prevails even in spring, summer, and fall.

Research on development in the hobbies and in volunteering is thinner than that in the amateur pursuits. The work that has been done shows a gradual pattern of involvement here in the crafts and woodworking activities (must acquire equipment, space, information, as in quilting, nature challenge hobbies, and the folk arts) (Stebbins, 1996; Stalp, 2007, pp. 61–63; Davidson & Stebbins, 2011). Casual observation also suggests development is gradual in most of the noncompetitive participatory activities and hobbyist sports and games.

Contingencies

There are also numerous career contingencies in the development stage. Joining a team, starting lessons, or entering a club, at least for minors, all require parental, moral, and financial support. To a significant degree, such support lies beyond the neophyte's control. The availability of appropriate teams, clubs, and lessons is also a contingency. For example, there are no football teams in Newfoundland; in certain fine arts, towns and small cities may lack qualified instructors; and science clubs may be scarce outside the larger centers. Often, too, children serious about a career in ballet must attend a special school in a faraway city (Sutherland, 1989, pp. 102–103). When the opportunity is available, however, in that it definitely has potential for changing the direction of the practitioner's career, this last contingency can actually become a contingent turning point. Another contingent turning point encountered at this time is the quality of the instruction received through coaching and private lessons.

Underlying these contingencies is still another: the access of would-be participants to credible information about the organizations providing the leisure (Fine, 1989). Boys, for example, must learn about the series of age-graded recreational leagues available in hockey, baseball, and football throughout much of North America. The football players I studied sometimes lacked this knowledge in their younger days.

As well, physical limitations may become contingencies, from the developmental stage on. For example, however appealing the thought, aspirants may lack the manual dexterity to play, even passably, the piano or violin. And neophytes may not have the sense of balance required for ballet, the size to play in the line in football, the agility to succeed at basketball. Note, too, that women are more likely than men to do the leg banding required in some ornithological research; their smaller hands and more delicate touch better equip them for the task. The barbershop study revealed the common practice in choruses of testing newcomers for their ability to carry a tune and hear harmonic intervals.

For amateurs, a more nebulous contingency at this career stage may involve finding opportunities to talk with professionals. Amateurs at all career stages enjoy rubbing elbows with their full-time counterparts, as long as the occasion is free of insults, snubs, condescension, and similar unpleasantnesses. At the developmental stage, salutary contact, because of its rarity, can be especially motivating. Professionals represent the highest expression of the activity that beginning amateurs dream of mastering. Chance encounters with such people can be inspiring; the amateur may run into a magnetic personality or see, at close range, a dazzling demonstration of technique or knowledge. In addition, accounts of a profession and its stars may give the amateur a sense of belonging to the activity's social world. Such encounters are also useful for amateurs who want to boast of their glamorous contacts to associates inside or outside the field.

Among the amateurs the beginner becomes proficient during the developmental stage of the amateur-professional career, possibly advancing far enough to reach the level of competence typical of the establishment stage. Each of the four areas of amateurism has a distinctive pathway of progress through development that is experienced as a subjective career. We turn first to art.

In general, progress during the developmental stage in art is manifested by the participant's growth of knowledge and ability – whether as a painter, musician, thespian, dancer, or writer – acquired through a combination of expert instruction, personal practice, and experience with public displays of one's art. The budding artist is taught, practices what he or she has learned, is evaluated, internalizes the evaluations, presents the art publicly, and is further evaluated. It is hoped that such a cycle brings about the requisite progress. Even in the amateur stage of development, there is, for the steadily improving practitioner, a more or less ascending set of prestigious opportunities to display one's artistic talents: exhibitions, recitals, competitions, and festivals, all organized by a range of sponsors (municipalities, conservatories, private teachers, public schools, charitable foundations).

In the group-based arts, such as dance, theater, and orchestral music, limited career progress is also possible through local advancement by way of a quasi-formal hierarchy. The improving violinist, for example, moves from section player to concertmaster in the university orchestra. The developing high school actress wins the lead in the class play. Groups may advance collectively as well, as in the youthful jazz band that finds increasingly better paying gigs, in more and more prestigious locations, for more and more refined audiences.

Sport is close to the fine arts in its pathway of progress during the developmental stage. Here progress is measured in terms of growing skill, however, gained from the combination of solitary practice, coaching or private instruction, and experience in competing against others. Formal knowledge is less important in sport than in fine art, where theories as to how to create art abound and often compete. Their nearest equivalent in sport may be the strategies used for trying to defeat competitors.

In amateur sport, as in art, there are ascending sets of prestigious opportunities for displaying talent: hierarchies of tournaments, leagues composed of club or school teams, meets, or competitions. Likewise, players can advance from reserve status to that of starter and, if exceptional, on to award winner (e.g., most valuable player, player of the week, member of the all-star team). Progress to this point in art and sport is much less contingent than it was in the beginning (though never is it wholly noncontingent). Now an artist's or player's own excellence is a major force in that person's career passage. Now there are turning points endowed with personal interpretations.

Because they almost always work alone, scientists and entertainers compared with artists and athletes share some common ground in the way they move through the developmental stage. Both may be characterized as *amateur-professional entrepreneurs* (Stebbins, 1980). These entrepreneurs turn up in such pursuits as golf, running, painting, sculpting, astronomy, archaeology, entomology, entertainment, creative writing, magic shows, singles tennis, and stand-up comedy. Other amateurs line up under what might be loosely called *avocational collectivism*. They are found in dance, football, baseball, hockey, theater, symphonic music, Broadway musicals, commercial dance music, and similar undertakings.

The differences between the entrepreneur and the collectivist in amateur-professional pursuits are manifested in the four dimensions of initiative, originality, independence, and risk (Stebbins, 1980). We turn, first, to these dimensions in entertainment, where entrepreneurship requires exceptional *initiative* to develop, promote, and perform an act in the highly competitive world of show business. Collective forms of entertainment, for example, professional hockey, commercial dance music, Broadway musicals, and dinner theater, deny their practitioners the opportunity to express self-reliance in this manner.

Originality must accompany initiative if the artist is to succeed as an entertainer. The act must have a novel twist to attract an audience and hold its attention. To be sure, originality is sometimes evident in some of the collective activities just mentioned, but it is less frequent there than in the variety arts. It is one thing to be asked to play an occasional spirited or moving solo as a member of an orchestra and quite another to do this regularly. If the audience is bored, an employer will refuse to book the comic in the future; meanwhile, the audience will spread the word about the performer's inadequacies. In contrast, the 'off-form' performance of a Broadway singer or actor on a particular night is hidden, to some extent, in the overall performance of the group.

As entrepreneurs, variety artists also have a considerable measure of *independence* in managing their affairs, once under way. Compare their situation with that of performers who must follow the dictates of a coach, conductor, or director. As well, variety artists assume *risks* to a degree unknown in collective entertainment. For example, stand-up comics promoted to opening spots seldom sign a contract with an agent that guarantees sufficient work to justify quitting their day job. Entertainment entrepreneurs do not necessarily invest more time, energy (emotional, physical), and money in their pursuits than others, but they do risk failure more often. Conversely, success is theirs and theirs alone, for they initiate and guide their interests without significant aid or support from others.

Scientists are entrepreneurs in much the same way. That is, they initiate their own research problems and the studies designed to solve them. Although replications are welcome in science, the overall emphasis is firmly on original contributions, on new data, theory, and research methods. In carrying out projects, scientists typically have a great deal of independence, an observation that is largely invalid, however, for research assistants and full-fledged scientists working in totalitarian circumstances. Finally, scientists, much like entertainers, assume risks. They court both success and failure. Indeed, the project may turn out well and advance knowledge in the discipline, or it may turn out poorly – the product of weak design, untenable hypotheses, or unforeseen circumstances.[7]

The amateur-professional entrepreneur gets started in the development stage of a career. But the entrepreneurial nature of the career continues and, indeed, is subject to enhancement through increased knowledge about, and experience with, the ways and means of taking initiative, being original, developing independence, and reducing risk. As described here, entrepreneurship is in fact a powerful magnet, pulling amateurs and professionals alike to science, entertainment, and the individual arts.

The entrepreneurial aspect of the amateur's life in art and entertainment does sometimes have a monetary element associated with it. During the development stage, this element is, in one sense, minor; amateurs make a living elsewhere from a job, not from an avocation whose remuneration is minuscule. But, in another sense, the first paid presentation of their art is very important – a major turning point at this time in their career.

There are at least four reasons for this interpretation. First, a fee symbolizes the attainment of a certain level of competence; it allows the amateur to claim to be a genuine practitioner rather than a mere neophyte. Second, the fact that someone is willing to pay for the amateur's creation is evidence of its value to others. It suggests, however tentatively, that one's talents and abilities have a certain level of public appeal. Third, it represents the first experience with a formal, contractual arrangement with a consumer or group of consumers in the area of one's art. When money changes hands, expectations change as well. Because of this payment, the artist is expected to produce what the consumer wants, on time, and at the agreed-upon fee. Fourth, the first paid performance may be the artist's first public performance, earlier ones having been given informally before friends or relatives. Developing entertainers find themselves in settings where the professionals in the field operate: at recording and television studios, in auditoriums, on stages, or anywhere before an audience that is expecting a performance. In such situations, the level of perfection expected is generally higher than that expected in informal settings.

Careers in volunteering

Leisure careers in volunteering are treated of separately here, primarily because we have little systematic research on the subject from which to make informed generalizations, however exploratory. Nevertheless, careers in this area are certainly possible. Consider some possibilities.

First, casual or project-based leisure volunteers might come to enjoy the experience and want to continue it through some related career volunteering. Consider, as an example, a woman who serves as a guide for a special exposition at the local zoo. On discovering that this instance of project-based leisure was most rewarding, she decides to sign up for training to become a docent, or (career) volunteer instructor on a particular animal, bird, or reptile held there in captivity.

Second, during my own lengthy experience as a volunteer, I have observed people assuming such career volunteer roles as member of a board of directors or president of a nonprofit organization. During their tenure in these positions, some of them discover their taste and aptitude for such responsibilities. Greatly enamored of this newfound way of using their free time, they seek at the end of their term, if not before, a similar high-level role in those third-sector areas of community life that appeal to them.

Third, I have observed people forced by circumstances to undertake nonwork obligations by, for example, reluctantly driving their children several times a week to practices, games, rehearsals, and performances in a sport or art. This routine does expose them to volunteer roles in these areas, however, and it may happen that one or two of those roles have considerable allure. The unpleasant obligation of furnishing transportation remains, but taking on the new voluntary, agreeable obligation sweetens that part of daily life while drawing the parent into the realm of genuine volunteering.

In these examples the newly minted career volunteer starts as a neophyte. As with other serious participants at this point in the leisure career, the later stages of establishment and development still lie before them. Further, note that career volunteers, if they start out in casual leisure, do not by definition dabble at those activities. Volunteering in casual leisure is a separate type (see Figure 2.1), wherein the participant altruistically serves a specified target of benefits. This service is not playfully given, but rather seriously provided. It is, however, seriously provided as unskilled, though needed, casual leisure requiring little or no technical knowledge (e.g., stuffing envelopes, distributing leaflets on a street corner).

Conclusion

The leisure career stages of beginning, development, and establishment encompass the period of time during which the participant is most likely to give up. For here there are bound to be costs. Here uncertainty is at its highest, while the rewards of the pursuit are weak compared with those that may come later in the maintenance stage. Embarrassment resulting from a substandard product or performance is often just around the corner. Expenses can also be discouraging, as in the costs of instruction, equipment, and perhaps memberships. And fulfilling pursuit of the activity during this period may prove to be too time-consuming, given other leisure interests and nonleisure responsibilities.

In short, an as-yet-unknown proportion of enthusiasts discover during these stages of their career in a new passion that such costs significantly outweigh its rewards and that they cannot stand to persevere until this ratio is reversed. The result is early abandonment of the activity. This practice remains to be systematically studied. Leisure abandonment at any stage is always a possibility (Stebbins, 2008), however, a process that has at least been conceptualized and will be considered late in the next chapter.

3
Amateurism as a Route to Fulfillment

The principal object of this chapter and the next two on the careers of hobbyists and career volunteers is to fill out in detail sufficient to demonstrate the nature of fulfillment in the first three career stages as found in a type of art, science, sport, or entertainment. In other words, what in particular do the fulfillment careers of, for instance, musicians, ornithologists, rugby players, and stand-up comics look like at the beginning and later in development and establishment? Discussion will, for the most part, be organized along lines of the six distinguishing qualities and the costs and rewards, all having been set out in Chapter 1. These basic internal conditions drive the fulfillment career. Fulfillment in the maintenance stage and its possible ebbing in decline are taken up in chapters 6 and 7, where we will also examine as amateur and hobbyist students in training for the professions and the trades.

Early careers in the fine arts

It makes sense in the study of careers in fine arts to treat separately the performing arts vis-à-vis those not intended for presentation on some sort of stage. The first is comprised of the musical, theatrical, and dance arts, whereas the second encompasses sculpting, literature, and the graphic arts.[1] Each of these five types has several subtypes. Moreover, every subtype is a highly complex entity of its own, exemplified most vividly by the rich texture of its professional wing. There is not sufficient space in a standard social science monograph to examine them all in the ethnographic detail characteristic of each.

Nonetheless, analysis according to the six qualities and several costs and rewards for the various subtypes will be all that is needed to paint an informative picture of the fulfillment careers of early amateurs and, later, of early hobbyists and volunteers.

Music

Amateur-professional fine art music consists, in the main, of five kinds: jazz (vocal, instrumental), choral singing, operatic singing, chamber music, and orchestral music. Pursuing a fulfilling career here entails persevering along the four dimensions of effort, skill, knowledge, and experience (i.e., the first three distinguishing qualities) on a musical instrument or the human voice. It is true, operatic singing is different from choral singing, just as playing jazz is different from playing classical music. But all rest on a shared set of acquirements that lead to good, hence fulfilling, musicianship.

In the beginning and development stages, these acquirements come with learning the rudiments of playing an instrument or singing and of reading and interpreting written music. In detail, this means learning the common musical scales, perfecting a sense of pitch (even on keyboards), developing a sense of timing, singing from the diaphragm, and learning to read music (e.g., notes, rests, interpretive symbols, and directives).

Budding jazz musicians learn in their development stage the basics of improvisation, an additional acquirement built on the foundation of these rudiments. In essence, these artists acquire an ever more sophisticated understanding of music theory and composition as expressed in jazz rhythms and the jazz idiom. They must now also learn rhythms rarely encountered outside jazz (e.g., funk, the Latin rhythms) and special scales such as the blues scale and the modal scales. On the classical side, the development stage is also the time for mastering the most commonly performed classical, chamber, choral, or operatic repertoire (including solos and solo passages) written for the amateur's instrument or vocal part (e.g., soprano, bass). In both jazz and classical music, participants must also become familiar with the conventional ways of performing certain pieces or works.

Most of this learning is achieved by way of routine instruction, practice, and performance, both public and private. Many music amateurs pass through the beginning and development stages guided primarily by a combination of private and group lessons and occasional performance opportunities available in the schools or the wider community (e.g., high school band, youth orchestra). Conservatory training in adolescence or early adulthood, specialized and concentrated as it is, accelerates progress through these first two stages toward that of establishment. By contrast, self-instruction – it is increasingly rare today – tends to retard this progress.

Nevertheless, experience (itself a kind of self-instruction) in the chosen music is vital, and musicians learn a great deal on the job, as it were. Gaining experience means, in part, gleaning the tricks of the trade of the art (Stebbins, 2014). The concept refers to the multitude of subtle maneuvers that facilitate good musicianship or constitute instances of it, but yet are rarely seen in the standard instructional package. School bands and youth orchestras may sporadically provide a few of them. But so do a diversity of informal sessions like busking (e.g., on street corners, in subways, *Economist*, 2013a), jazz jam sessions (e.g., in after-hour joints, someone's home), chamber music gatherings (usually in someone's home), and, somewhat more formally, workshops. Gleaning the tricks of the trade is crucial to every fulfillment career, and for this reason the process will be considered throughout this book.

Establishment

As mentioned, musicians enter the establishment stage when they believe they have sufficiently mastered the basics of their instrument and their music. In general, the goal is to find a place in the amateur or professional world; in a word, to become established in their pursuit. This process differs for amateurs and professionals, although, to varying degrees, it is at times stressful for both.

The line between developing as a performing artist and becoming established as one is much hazier for the amateur than the professional. At a point late in development, amateurs begin to routinize the pursuit of their activity in their particular locale. This process involves finding and cultivating opportunities to play or sing, which is always significantly shaped by the amount of available free time for and level of interest in pursuing those opportunities. This highly personal ratio was considered earlier, in more general terms, under the heading of the seriousness dimension of involvement. Now, in establishment and maintenance, the need to remain in practice waxes ever stronger, for such opportunities are often competitive and finding exceptional ones are notable turning points.

As for the social world of the amateur's instrumental or vocal specialty, involvement in it arrives quickly for the neophyte. Very soon the typical beginner establishes relationships with one or more of the following: an instructor, music supplier and, for instrumentalists, an instrument sales and repair service. Expansion of this social world continues in the development stage. Now participants seek exemplars of their chosen music, in general, and their instrument or vocal part, in particular. In practice, this means patronizing CD and DVD vendors (whether online or in brick-and-mortar shops), going to concerts and other performances, watching special shows on television, and the like. Being substantially influenced by one or more of these exemplars – now considered role models – is itself a turning point (e.g., a junior cellist or jazz vocalist heavily influenced by Pablo Casals or Ella Fitzgerald, respectively).

Starting late in development and spreading across the stage of establishment, a further expansion of the musician's social world typically occurs. Amateurs pursue their passions steadily, which in music requires finding one or more dependable outlets for playing or singing. Personal agency is paramount here. The budding artist bent on succeeding must aggressively seek opportunities to perform and learn. Jam sessions and chamber sessions enable this, although they foster little contact with the general public. Rather, public contact comes with, for instance, performing in the occasional concert, playing sporadically or regularly in a nightclub or restaurant, singing or playing in church, and so on. This public and the events themselves are also part of the musician's social world. At this point in the music career, these involvements are commonly mediated by an informal network of contacts: amateurs are invited to play with others whom they have met in the past.

It is during establishment that musicians come to grips with professionalization, with whether to try to make money and, if oriented thus, whether to try to make enough to gain a livelihood or at least contribute significantly to one. Throughout this period of uncertainty, the musician's social world expands still further. For it is at this time that musicians get involved with impresarios, broadly defined here as any person or agency who engages their services, gratis or remunerated.[2]

Identity, especially as expressed in reputation for musicianship, is a crucial consideration in establishment. More broadly, is the musician competent, cooperative, reliable, and genial? Without such a reputation, amateurs may find others being invited to join a group instead of themselves. It is during the course of getting known, of developing a positive reputation, that amateurs may face significant stress (a cost of serious leisure). Being well respected along these lines also helps confirm the participant's personal identity as amateur musician.

At what point does an amateur turn professional? For many musicians, this happens when they find enough work in music to allow them to experience another turning point or, as the saying goes, 'to quit their day job'. By the time, this is a realistic option routinizing involvement is at most a minor concern. There are now a decent number of opportunities to play in a typical week, suggesting that the reputation of these musicians on the music-related job market is solid. Now their goal is to find work that is ever more agreeable and prestigious. This search may be conducted locally, regionally, nationally, even internationally, depending on how their musical interest is organized (e.g., community orchestras, traveling jazz bands, traveling choral groups) and how willing they are to work away from home. We explore in Chapter 6 the kinds of livelihoods that professional musicians typically generate.

The role of parents

The reaction of parents to their children's intention to find their life-work in art or entertainment is an important force mediating career passage from amateur to professional. Research suggests that parents are particularly uneasy about their children's decision to seek a career in entertainment and, depending on the field and the sex of offspring, even in art and sport (Stebbins, 1990; 1993b). Women starting careers in professional golf and tennis, for example, are usually encouraged by their parents (Theberge, 1977; Kutner, 1983). In contrast, artists of both sexes face noticeable parental opposition when they announce their intention to earn a living from art (Simpson, 1981, pp. 54–56).

Some parental opposition roots in stereotypes. Certain arts, among them ballet and theater, and many entertainment fields (e.g., magic, stand-up comedy) are supposedly home to weird, unsavory, or deviant people. Such occupations are held to be rife with unmanageable contingencies (including favoritism) and plagued by low or erratic income. Nightclub work is especially scorned for daughters, who are often defined as too pure for routine association with the patrons of such places. Furthermore, parents may regard sport and entertainment as trivial, a 'cute' diversion of young amateurs who, with the announcement of professional interests, are seen as having got out of hand. Thus, early in the establishment stage, parental resistance can be a career contingency to reckon with.

But there are sons and daughters who persevere against these attitudes (as noted, later they resist abandoning their pursuit). And, my research suggests, their parents tend eventually to come onside, which is most likely to occur after the former have been able to demonstrate how deeply fulfilling their work can actually be. That it may be relatively less remunerative than some other occupations may also have subsided as a parental worry by the time the young artist is reasonably established.

Theater and dance

I include under the heading of fine art theater that classified as experimental, classical, mime, and art cinematic production. The experimental and classical types are performed on the amateur level as community theater. In dance, the main breakdown is ballet and modern, both offering a number of subtypes. And, though the fit is not perfect, figure skating in its artistic manifestation is conceived of as dancing on ice.

The beginnings

Dabbling is a possible precursor in all theater save cinematic production, but only in the sense that the dabblers are playing at presenting a brief sketch. It is substantially improvised (in script and bodily movements), often utilizing a handful of locally available props. Children seem especially attracted to this genre of casual leisure. A budding thespian might develop a taste for theater by way of such enjoyment, but considerable preliminary instruction would be necessary even to begin to act in experimental or classical theater or in mime – that is, to become a neophyte. The minimal requirements for the first two include an ability to read the script, align the words with appropriate gestures and stage business, and coordinate one's part with those of the other actors onstage.[3] As for mime, getting started presupposes considerable basic knowledge of how to perform it, as the wikiHow Web site on the subject demonstrates so well (http://www.wikihow.com/Mime, retrieved 30 March 2013). It seems improbable that anyone would try to dabble at this art.

The same goes for cinematic production. At the least, neophytes must first learn how to use a camera to the point of being able to capture on film or digital camera the scenario they (possibly in collaboration with others) have created. Already, this is a serious undertaking, quite unlike spontaneous hammering on a piano or playing with a paint brush or sketching pencil.

Ballet is another art that discourages dabbling, if not rendering it impossible. Before neophytes progress at all they must master several rudimentary bodily postures and foot and leg positions. To accomplish this, requires specialized flexibility and strengthening of critical muscles in different parts of the body.[4] Since an ability to skate necessarily precedes playful attempts at figure skating, entry-level dabbling also seems out of the question here. One might dabble at modern dance, however, it having been born early in the 20th century in reaction to the artistic rigidity of traditional ballet. Here dancers are encouraged to design their own steps and routines. Modern dance is also characterized by whole-body movements, use of gravity, and body weight, which includes falling to the floor. Seeing tantalizing displays on television or onstage, for instance, could conceivably trigger some dabbling in certain admirers.

Perreault (1988), who studied a large sample of dancers of various kinds in Quebec, found that men came to dancing by accident. They had to take a course in it as part of a theater specialty in university, a complement to gymnastics, or a form of exercise for certain sports. By contrast women were inspired by their parents, friends, or images of dance they viewed in the media. Perrault observed that, initially, the stereotype that ballet is a female activity clearly influenced the men.

Development

As with music the program of development – the road to fulfillment – that greets the neophyte in theater and dance is quickly established when that person enters the art. The beginning ballet dancer, once having learned the five basic positions must, now in development, practice them to perfection or near perfection. With this comes increased muscle strength and sense of balance. The same may be said for developing figure skaters (McQuarrie & Jackson, 1996). In theatrical development, beginners will learn, among many other things, how to interpret the scripts they can now read and how to integrate their spoken lines with their gestures and stage business. They will also learn about, for example, voice projection and enunciation of words, about eye contact and facial expressions.

In these arts a rudimentary social world soon takes shape for the beginner and continues evolving through development. Here, too, the teacher – in private lessons, group instruction (often in dance studios) – is an essential early part of this world. In ballet and figure skating the supplier of shoes, skates, and clothing constitutes another crucial initial part. As dancers, skater, and actors get better, many will participate with others in formal productions of their art, thereby putting them in contact with directors, costume personnel, make-up artists, and the like. Last, but not least, are their colleagues, their coparticipants, who are usually at the same career stage. By the end of development the social world of actors, skaters, and dancers, especially those who perform with others, has expanded considerably. Part of being such an artist is to be recognized by its insiders as a proper member of this exclusive formation.

So here, too, the fulfillment career advances along the lines of growing skill, knowledge, and experience fired by the effort that these participants make toward achieving such development. Sutherland (1989, p. 99) says that, unlike in other occupations and professions, ballet dancers in their teens must make a conscious decision to get 'serious' about the art. This turning point signals entry into stage of establishment.

Establishment

The passion for dance, drama, or figure skating now firmly rooted the increasingly vital question is how to routinize involvement. Early in establishment in these arts this commonly means regularly trying out for community theater or dance productions or, in figure skating, passing tests of skills and succeeding in competitive events.

Meeting and possibly even working with professional actors can be a major contingency during establishment in theater. Community theaters sometimes hire one or more professional to play key roles in certain plays. Perry and Carnegie (2013) studied a pro-am theater project in Britain, wherein amateurs and professionals worked collaboratively. They performed together in the same production and sometimes the pros mentored a full cast of amateurs.

In ballet, professionally oriented beginners learn their art in 'community ballet' programs, possibly advancing within them to the point where they are taken on as (often unpaid) apprentices or trainees in a ballet company. That company may well be local, and it uses the community program as a recruitment pool. Apprentices who make the grade may then be invited into that company's corps de ballet, a remunerated position, although often at starting salaries too low for a full-time livelihood (Wakin, 2007). This is a significant turning point.

It is different, of course, for the pure amateurs. Daniel Wakin (2007) observes that, among the amateur performing arts, ballet is the most physically demanding. Nevertheless, this fails to deter its *passionnés*:

> Yet a substratum of dedicated – even fanatical – amateurs does exist. They give small recitals at studios or work with teachers to create a dance and have it videotaped. Others who become advanced take part in small-town 'Nutcracker' performances.[5] Many women and men become dedicated class-takers, often mingling in open classes with professional dancers. Teachers of adults acquire devoted followers.

Modern dance amateurs at this stage typically find routine opportunities within a dance studio, commonly the one in which they developed from the beginning. Performing dance companies formed strictly for amateurs (they operate like community orchestras) seem to exist only in the largest cities. Further, some amateur modern dancers augment this routine by entering various dance competitions.

Establishment is chiefly an adult concern in figure skating. It entails routinely preparing for and entering skating competitions organized by local skating clubs or those organized on a regional or national basis by more inclusive organizations. These competitions are commonly age-graded and may also be restricted to a particular level of skill (e.g., masters competitions).

The individual fine arts

The graphic arts make up one category of these pursuits, a diverse group encompassing calligraphy, photography, drawing, painting, printmaking, lithography, typography, serigraphy (silk-screen printing), and bookbinding. Sculpting, carving, and molding of clay, wood, metal, wire, or putty constitute a second category known as the plastic arts. The third category is literature, composed mainly of fiction, nonfiction, and poetry.

Dabbling is out of the question in those individual arts requiring specialized equipment or resources the effective use of which requires a significant amount of instruction. It is thus with photography, printmaking, lithography, typography, serigraphy, and bookbinding. Computer-based graphic design is included in this generalization, since the programs enabling it must be learned and applied. By contrast, one may dabble at painting, drawing, and calligraphy and, given the raw materials, at sculpting, carving, and molding. And people with an ordinary literary competence may nevertheless try their hand, untrained, at the three kinds of literature.

As neophytes the nondabbling individual artists learn their art through one or a combination of formal instruction, group or private; self-direction based on instructional material found in bookstores and online; or manuals accompanying the equipment and supplies (e.g., cameras, calligraphy kits, sculpting kits). Those dabblers who are inclined to get 'serious' about their play – to become neophytes – head in the same direction, toward formal or self-directed instruction, if not some of both. All the individual arts discussed here lend themselves to personal instruction, as evidenced by the multitude of manuals presently on the book market (see Amazon.com). Adult education courses on these activities are also plentiful.

In taking formal courses, the beginning individual artists immediately enter the social world of their art, accomplished by forming relationships with an instructor and possibly some students. Furthermore, both formally and informally trained beginners must soon contact sellers of needed equipment and supplies. Later, both types usually want to show others what they have produced, to display, for example, their serigraphic, photographic, or literary works.

During development the skill–knowledge–experience base of individual artists continues to expand.[6] The club is arguably the most common organizational structure that nurtures this growth. These artists typically produce their art alone, but join one or more clubs to display it, pick up tips about doing it, and generally be part of the local scene that has sprung up around their art. And, as these artists improve, they may want to enter their products in local expositions and competitions. Here they meet the organizers of these events as well as other amateur participants and members of the public. All these contacts enlarge still further the social world of the individual artist.

Research on the amateur careers of the individual fine artists is rare and, with one exception, none has been guided by the SLP. That exception is Ailsa's Craig's (2007) study of poets, in which she traces their passage across the different stages of career discussed in this book.[7] Her work demonstrates well the precariousness of careers in the fine arts. She observed that poets often drift into their profession, in effect dabbling at poetry as children and adolescents.

Getting established

Late development shades imperceptibly into establishment as the individual artists get into their stride of routinely pursuing their passion. In establishment, they arrive at a schedule composed of hours, days, and weeks wherein they practice their craft. For some of them, regularly occurring expositions and competitions are part of this schedule. Further, winning a major award on these occasions is a momentous turning point. Engaging in their art is now a clear part of their leisure lifestyle. And for those testing the winds for a possible professional career, there is the ever-present need to find a paying market for their products. For these enthusiasts, getting established entails identifying and profiting in that market.

I could find no research on the role of parents in the lives of individual artists. Perhaps that is at it should be, for most of these arts are usually taken up, at the earliest, in late adolescence. Nonetheless, painting, drawing, sculpting, molding (e.g., using Play-Doh), and carving (e.g., soap, wood) do appeal to some children, and some parents might conceivably become anxious at the thought that Johnnie or Susie might be interested in adopting one of them as his or her life work.[8] In any case, being a reasonably accomplished author, photographer, sculptor, or calligrapher is a powerful source of identity, whether amateur or professional.

Early careers in the entertainment arts

Although most people are unaware of the following generalization or, if they are, sometimes have difficulty accepting its validity, it is nevertheless true that, with few exceptions, the entertainment arts are founded on their counterparts in the fine arts.[9] Thus, the stand-up comic is an actor, the country fiddler a musician, the pop novelist a writer, and the commercial artist a painter or drawer. That is, to succeed in their entertainment art, these amateurs/professionals must learn the basic techniques and principles of their foundational art, the same ones their fine arts colleagues must learn.

The following list of entertainment arts is incomplete, since it contains only those with professional wings holding great appeal for amateurs. Entertainment music is composed mainly of rock and its derivatives, country, and commercial folk music. Dancing as entertainment may be classified as follows: jazz, choral or show, ballroom, tap, and country.[10] Theater designed to be entertaining includes: commercial community (musical, operetta, comedy, drama), entertainment mime, entertainment magic, commercial cinematic production (including home film and video), stand-up comedy, sketch, puppetry, public speaking, and sundry variety arts (mainly juggling, clowning, ventriloquism, and acrobatics). All the individual arts of painting and literature have their purely entertaining counterparts. Drawing, for example, amuses through cartoons and caricatures.

Amateurs abound in both the fine arts and the entertainment fields. This concentration may be traced in no small measure to the difficulty of finding work in them, work sufficiently remunerative to sustain even a half decent living. Put otherwise, such a living can only be possible when combined with steady part-time employment in another occupation. The enormous appeal of performing or presenting an entertainment or fine art when, as today, its job market is languishing in the arid climate of the Information Age throws open the gates of these fields to massive amateur participation (Carrier, 1995).

While dabbling is largely impossible in any of the entertainment fields mentioned above, self-directed instruction is abundantly available there (see Amazon.com for long lists of books in each art). The beginning and development stages are commonly filled with reading, observing more experienced artists, asking questions of some of them, trial-and-error learning sequences, and the like. These instructional strategies suck the beginner into the art's social world. In implementing them, this person gains access to the 'scene', as by going back stage, hanging out after hours, frequenting brick-and-mortar sales outlets (e.g., magic shops, musical instrument suppliers), and joining some of the helpful online organizations and services.

Self-directed instruction in the entertainment arts may be sought in parallel with formal training. On the formal level, schools, programs, workshops, and the like are available in each, often promoted in the Yellow Pages and online under the heading of the entertainment or variety arts. The beginning and development stages of the entertainment arts careers are characterized by learning from these formal and informal sources.

In establishment these artists, as amateurs or budding professionals, persevere in finding routine outlets for their talents. Here, too, personal agency is a major asset. Some open their own commercial services, offering entertaining acts for parties, conventions, meetings, and so on. Here, as earlier, lies the challenge of making enough money to go professional, if in fact that is the artist's goal. Those on the professional path may sign with a booking agency, which can be a turning point.

Early careers in sport

As in the arts it is illuminating to treat sport according to whether it is team-based or individual-based. Bearing in mind that amateur sport is defined, in part, by the fact that it has a professional counterpart, Tables 3.1 and 3.2 reasonably exemplify team and individual activities. Those marked with an asterisk (*) are also elite-amateur sports and also featured in the Olympic Games and other major international athletic contests. Here, in some countries, the amateur's livelihood may be provided by public or private funds, if not both, as well as by possible commercial endorsements. In many countries, however, Olympians and the like receive little or no funding, even paying their own way to the games in which they compete. Note

Table 3.1 Team sports

Amateur	Elite-amateur
Football	Field hockey
Basketball*	Yachting
Baseball	Bobsledding
Ice hockey*	Volleyball
Soccer*	Rowing
Rugby	Water polo
Cricket	Synchronized swimming
Roller hockey	

Table 3.2 Individual sports

Amateur	Elite-amateur
Boxing*	Handball
Tennis (including doubles)	Swimming
Golf	Diving
Squash	Track and field events
Racquetball (including doubles)	Archery
Jai alai (including doubles)	Badminton (including doubles)
Equestrian events*	Martial arts
Bowling	Speed skating
Figure skating (including pairs)*	Alpine skiing and snowboarding
Auto racing	Cross-country skiing
Motorcycle racing	Ski jumping
Rodeo (calf roping, steer wrestling, bull riding, etc.)	Cycling
Bodybuilding	Shooting (fire arms)
	Weight lifting
	Gymnastics
	Canoe and kayak racing
	Luge
	Fencing
	Sailing
	Wrestling

that bodybuilding also has its hobbyist side, which will be touched on in the next chapter.

A key inspiration for seriously taking up a particular sport is an enduring passion for the game itself, possibly fired equally by a powerful attraction for its 'equipment,' as in a love of horses or dogs used in competitive events (Baldwin & Norris, 1999; Chevalier, Le Mancq, & Simonet, 2011). Still, not everyone is crazy about competitive play in, for instance, football, hockey, badminton, kayaking, or alpine skiing.[11] But, for those for whom their sport is a passion, they may have started in it by dabbling. This is possible in nearly all the sports listed in the two tables, with fencing, rodeo, and ski jumping appearing among the few exceptions. Many a serious amateur and professional athlete got started by casually throwing a ball, splashing around in a swimming pool, riding a bicycle, and the like (Borden, 2013). Most dabblers stop here. But those who become neophytes have parents who encouraged them or gave in to their demands to find instruction and, where appropriate, be allowed to join a team.

In this regard, female boxing stands out. Lucia Trimbur (2013, pp. 95–96) found in her sample of women who boxed at Gleason's Gym in New York that early interests in the sport were chiefly practical. Some entered it as a way of reclaiming their body and gaining a sense of empowerment following a violent romantic relationship. Others sought training in self-defense. A third group wrestled with eating disorders, unhealthy exercise habits, or risky lifestyles. Love for the sport per se was not a motivating sentiment for this group.

In the team sports, rudimentary instruction in technique is commonly provided by one or more coaches. Here, participants also learn about the structure of the game and its rules. Those going in for an individual sport typically learn it by way of personal lessons or specialized courses, sometimes both. Team or individual, this formal learning is augmented by informal advice given on the spot by more experienced peers and found in, books, magazines, and online sources. Third, the developing athlete learns from observing peers and professionals, as they appear in live, televised, and video-taped matches and in workshops.[12]

For the committed effort, perseverance, and the acquisition of skill and knowledge are of utmost importance throughout. Thus, sport tends to be physically demanding, even though shooting and auto and motorcycle racing are much less so. Skill and knowledge get expressed through experience, often held to be the best teacher. As in the arts, gaining experience in a sport means, in part, gleaning its tricks of the trade. Additionally, some experience is manifested in simply reacting unthinkingly though effectively to common situations that spring up in sporting contests.

Participation in elite-amateur sport may be conceived of as taking place in the late establishment/early maintenance stages of the fulfillment career. Athletes at this level usually play at their maximum physical ability, as established by genetic endowment, acquired skills, and applicable knowledge. For these reasons, careers here are relatively short, though in figure skating, the elite-amateur phase may become a springboard for a subsequent career in professional entertainment. Now, artistic performance will take precedence over the punishing displays of technique required earlier in competition. The rest, if Pawluk's (1984) research on retired Polish Olympians is representative, tend after further higher education to take up high-status, non-sports-related jobs.

The social worlds of the various sports are typically highly evolved. Those of beginners start to take shape around a team or instructor, depending on whether the sport is collective or individual. But very soon critical purveyors of equipment, clothing, and repair services join the formation. Like-minded friends and relatives compose another part of this world, as do the people who make up an external public. These elements blend with the organization of competitive opportunities: leagues of teams, schedules of matches, regular and special tournaments, championship play-offs, and more. Players in establishment may also have sporadic contact with the sports media, while those interested in going professional are commonly in contact with scouts, possibly an agent as well.

The player's parents occupy a special place in this social world. First, they are a significant part of that person's public. Second, they may help the player financially. Third, they may encourage entering the sport and assiduously practicing to succeed in it. Still, when it comes to a possible professional career, not all parents favor it, it appears. Since most sports are physically demanding – shooting and auto and motorcycle racing being least so – such careers as just noted are short. McPherson, Curtis, and Loy (1989, p. 261) observe that professional athletes often retire before 30 years of age and that physical decline commonly figures into their decision to this. Consequently, parents may fret about what lies ahead economically and socially, once the glamor and money common at the top of much of pro sport are no longer available.[13]

Early careers in science

Though the amateurs in science wind up being researchers, the conditions prodding them in this direction are different. That is, as pointed out in Chapter 2, there is commonly some profound emotional attachment to the subject of inquiry. The desire to contribute scientifically to it is a special expression of this fascination. These are the pure scientific amateurs. The student amateurs in training for a devotee work career are considered in Chapter 6.

My research on serious leisure involvements in science revealed three kinds of participants: observers, armchair participants, and applied scientists.[14] The observers are amateurs; they directly experience their objects of interest through scientific inquiry. The armchair participants are liberal arts hobbyists who pursue their interests largely, if not wholly, through reading (more on them in the next chapter). They hold to their approach either because they prefer it to observation or because they lack the time, equipment, opportunity, or physical stamina to go into the field or laboratory. The applied scientists, who are also amateurs, express their knowledge of a branch of science in some practical way. As far as we know, the most active group of applied amateurs is found in computer science.

Amateur observers vary much more than their professional counterparts in their level of knowledge and degree of willingness and ability to contribute original data to their science. Thus the observers pursue their scientific activity as one of three subtypes referred to here as apprentices, journeymen, and masters.[15] Further, some of them find that their leisure career in their science has them advancing from apprentice to journeyman and possibly on to master.[16] Such passage is an inexact process, however, for the acquisition of knowledge, experience, and personal confidence is always gradual and at times hesitant.

Scientific apprentices are beginners (neophytes). They hope to absorb enough about their discipline, its research procedures, and its instrumentation to function as journeymen and eventually, perhaps, as masters. As their knowledge about their science grows, some apprentices specialize, becoming beginners here as well. Scientific apprentices, unlike their opposite number in the trades, are normally independent; formal association with a master over a prescribed period of time is unheard of. Even at this stage, these practitioners have the freedom to explore their science on their own, which they do mostly by reading and listening to talks. At this point, however, they are typically incapable of making an original contribution to it.

Journeymen are knowledgeable, reliable practitioners who can work independently in one or a few specialties. They have advanced far enough to make original contributions to their science and, in this capacity having passed through development, are working at the establishment stage of their career. Yet, it is a matter of personal definition as to whether an amateur has reached this level of expertise. The amateurs I interviewed were typically modest, even humble, about their attainments. They seemed to sense when they were effectively apprentices, when they had much to learn, and when they needed supervision in, say, excavating an archaeological site or needed more experience in working up a valid set of observations. Even journeymen may feel 'inadequate' after comparing themselves with the local professionals with whom a number of them have frequent contact. Journeymen are always learning, expanding their grasp of the discipline as a whole, and absorbing new developments pertaining to their specialties. The same holds for the masters as well as the professionals.

The masters actually contribute to their science, most often by collecting original data on their own that help advance the field. They operate in late establishment and throughout maintenance. They are aware of certain knowledge gaps in their specialties, and they know how to make the observations that can conceivably close or at least narrow those gaps. To this end, they systematically collect the relevant data and publicize them through talks, reports, and journal articles.[17] Any amateur can contribute through serendipity such as by fortuitously discovering a new celestial object. But masters systematically seek new data through programs they design (e.g., digging their own archaeological sites) or coordinate with others (e.g., working as part of a team spread across the country to observe a lunar occultation).[18]

Master amateur research projects are chiefly exploratory and descriptive, however, with the theorizing and hypotheses-testing being left to the pros. Nevertheless, when these projects are properly carried out, validation of the researcher's status as a master follows. Amateurs and professionals alike acknowledge the individual's contributions, journal articles are accepted for publication, and the occasional local speaking invitation may even be received.

In principle, every science can have an amateur wing, for no science formally restricts data collection within its domain. Yet, as the following list demonstrates, only some sciences have a formally established amateur component. It is probable that the others effectively, though inadvertently, discourage amateur participation. This they do by being highly abstract or by requiring equipment or training largely inaccessible to nonprofessionals. The following sciences have active amateur wings and, in harmony with the preceding discussion, are primarily exploratory and descriptive. Moreover, each has local variations in its objects of study so extensive that its professional core needs help to cover them all. Here, the amateurs in the area are keen to lend a hand.

Physical sciences

Physics
Computer science
Astronomy
Mineralogy
Meteorology

Biological sciences

Ornithology
Entomology
Botany

Social sciences

History
Archaeology
Geography (cartography)

Reading in a science and collecting descriptive data on one of its relevant research problems are two core activities in these amateur pursuits. Amateurs in physics are concentrated in the branch of upper atmosphere or space physics where they explore the radio waves as ham radio operators. Amateurs in computer science explore the applications of the latest hardware and software available for personal computers. Amateurs in astronomy describe meteor showers, stellar and lunar occultations, variable star activity, and other celestial phenomena. Those in mineralogy study the nature and distribution of rocks and minerals in a particular geographic area, usually the one where they live.

Amateurs in meteorology participate in local weather forecasting. In ornithology, they systematically observe the behavior and habitats of birds. Latter career specialization has been studied extensively in this activity, as in observing only certain kinds of birds perhaps at only certain locations (Scott, Ditton, Stoll, & Eubanks, 2005). Amateur entomologists do much the same, focusing instead on insects. Amateur botanists collect, identify, and preserve specimens of various kinds of plant life found in a given geographic area.

Amateur historians nearly always write in the branch of their discipline known as local history, typically concentrating on their own town or region. It is likewise for amateur archaeologists, who search for prehistoric relics and sites of human use and habitation, describing and preserving what they find. Amateur, or 'citizen', cartographers use various new technologies such as mapping apps, GPS-enabled smart phones, other handheld GPS devices, Google maps, and OpenStreetMap to plot a (usually) local service, kind of retail outlet, annoying municipal problem, and the like (Diep, 2011). In most of the fields listed here, the amateurs follow the lead of their professional counterparts and specialize, as in the study of song birds, binary stars, or mushrooms (mycology). This is not true, however, for amateur cartography.

The background knowledge needed for a career in amateur science comes from a variety of sources, most of which require the participant to read published material. Beginners take credit and noncredit courses, which combine reading and lectures and are often available in the aforementioned sciences at colleges and universities throughout the West. In addition, articles bearing on different specialties are published from time to time in periodicals intended for the amateur market of these disciplines. Finally, the amateurs, possibly in collaboration with one or more local professionals, may establish a local club. Here they meet as often as weekly for workshops, reports on research by their colleagues, and the occasional lecture delivered by a professional.

Even though apprentices hardly gain their knowledge overnight, they seem to progress more quickly to the stage of journeyman than the other types of amateurs mentioned in this chapter progress to an equivalent stage in their fields. For the latter, compared with acquiring intellectual knowledge, more time is needed to polish physical skills and harness them according to the appropriate principles of implementation. As a reasonable estimate it takes approximately six months for the typical amateur scientist to reach establishment and the level of scientific journeyman.

Social world

The local club, which may be a chapter of a national organization, forms part of the core of the typical amateur scientist's social world. This core is further constituted of the places where research is conducted (e.g., excavation sites in archaeology, forests in ornithology, and archives and libraries in local history). And since amateur science is intellectual work, a home study of some sort is indispensable and is therefore another core space in this social world. The master amateurs and the professionals of the science inhabit the center of this world. Within this nucleus, these amateurs collect data for the pros who use them either to generate new propositions about the object of study or to test existing hypotheses bearing on it. The social world of amateur science also has a number of important peripheral members, notably equipment vendors and journal editors.

What makes all the amateur social worlds truly distinct is that professionals play so a central role in them. In most instances, they are locally available so the amateurs may rub elbows with them, pattern their scientific lives after them, and marvel at their feats made possible by full-time devotion to the activity. Although not all professionals are good role models or blessed with agreeable personalities, a sufficient number of them come close enough to these ideals to win a place of honor in one of the worlds of avocational science. They may only rarely be seen in person, but their influence is both wide and deep, in part because of their frequent appearance in the discipline's print and electronic media.

It is the absence of this professional counterpart that most clearly distinguishes hobbyists from amateurs. Nevertheless, looking solely at the former, this condition should never be misunderstood as a mark of inferiority, simplicity, or triviality. As will become evident in the next chapter, no serious leisure hobby can be described in such terms.

Career contingencies and abandonment

Leisure abandonment is a point in the fulfillment career at which the individual leaves a particular leisure activity. The antecedent conditions of abandonment are at the same time negative career contingencies and the five resulting types of abandonment are simultaneously types of these contingencies. Furthermore, contingencies when they arise force the participant to adjust to them. Abandoning the activity in question is one such adjustment, albeit the ultimate one. Other adjustments enable that person to continue in the serious pursuit. Abandonment and adjustment signal that career paths in the serious pursuits are by no means always linear, leading steadily toward ever greater fulfillment (for a detailed discussion of this pattern, see Backlund & Kuentzel, 2013).

Abandoning a serious pursuit is momentous. My observations to date suggest that this is accomplished by way of one of the following alternatives: (1) deciding consciously to quit the activity, (2) being forced from it by external circumstances, or (3) leaving the activity by drifting away from it. The activity, be it casual, serious, or project-based leisure, has been pursued long enough for the participant to have developed a positive, reasonably strong emotional attachment to it, such as that felt in enjoyment or fulfillment (see Stebbins, 2008). And this sentimental state holds even if the attachment has faded somewhat, as happens in Alternative 3. Abandonment of a serious leisure activity is at the same moment the final turning point in the participant's leisure career in the activity. And whereas enthusiasts leaving their activities by way of Alternatives 1 and 2 could conceivably become reunited with them, that possibility appears at the time of abandonment to be both far away and most improbable. In short, the experience of abandonment is usually poignant enough to amount to a personal crisis of sorts.

This section on contingencies as linked to abandonment will be limited to those occurring in the serious pursuits. Both are possible at any stage of the fulfillment career, with parts of the following discussion applying as much to the neophyte as to someone in maintenance or decline. The contingency/abandonment focus is on what is 'wrong' with a current activity and may want to leave it – rather than on the allure of another activity, whether as replacement, substitute, addition, or a way of meeting a 'leisure lack' (Stebbins, 2008, p. 14). A problem unique to the contingency/abandonment process is that, especially in the serious pursuits but also to some extent in the project-based form, leaving is personally decisive. For this is renunciation of leisure, of a pursuit founded on substantial commitment to its core activity as well as on a set of deeply fulfilling rewards derived from it. Why would a participant want to give up such activity? What has gone wrong?

Contingencies leading to career abandonment

The negative career contingencies and adjustment to them by way of leisure abandonment, which to my knowledge have never been systematically examined in the leisure sciences, whether under these headings or their equivalent, can be enormously varied and complex. What is more, it appears that most people face these contingencies and possible abandonment at least once during their fulfillment career. So far, based on sporadic instances of them observed in my own research, I have been able to identify 13 contingencies capable of inciting abandonment. Together they compose 5 types:

Motivational contingencies

1. Participant loses interest in the activity.
2. Participant retains interest, but an even more appealing activity comes along, leading the person to abandon the first one. This assumes that to pursue both activities would require more time or money, or both, than is available.

Social psychological contingencies

3. Participant is faced with social pressures largely beyond personal control.

4. Participant is faced with social psychological pressures largely beyond personal control.
5. Participant is faced with a lack of crucial social support.

Physical contingencies

6. Participant suffers long-term injury or illness.
7. Participant suffers irremediable injury or illness.
8. Participant experiences debilitating physical or mental changes attendant on aging.

Geographic contingencies

9. Participant is faced with enduring changes in enabling geographic conditions.

Regulatory contingencies

10. Participant is faced with regulations that set insurmountable limits.
11. Participant is accused of alleged or proved behavior considered unacceptable by others.
12. Participant is faced with insurmountable competitive arrangements.
13. Participant is accused of a legally or morally suspect maneuver.

This is a fair list, but even then probably not an exhaustive one. Nevertheless, it is long enough to give us a cornucopia of examples with which to flesh out the rudiments of the contingency/abandonment framework.

Motivational contingencies

Here leisure abandonment occurs when a person consciously decides to participate no further in the activity. This was the type that first alerted me to the broader issue of leisure abandonment, as just set out. It is also the most perplexing of the five types, since it raises the question of why people abandon certain highly attractive activities. Indeed, Contingency 1 seems to have no facile explanation.

I dealt with this contingency in my comparison of devotee work and serious leisure (Stebbins, 2004c/2014). There I observed that some people eventually come realize that their formerly highly appealing work or leisure is no longer nearly as enjoyable and fulfilling as it once was. It has become too humdrum, possibly no longer offering sufficient challenge, novelty, or social reward (e.g., social attraction, group accomplishment, contribution to development of a larger collectivity). Perhaps they have become discouraged with one or more of its core tasks, so discouraged that they believe they will never again find deep satisfaction here. Extensive bias against the participant such as in judging, player selection, and favoritism can sap motivation.

Contingency 2 centers on the fact of having found a new leisure activity that, by comparison, makes the current one look substantially less attractive. And this even when the current activity has none of the 'faults' just described (i.e., being humdrum and the like). As for the so-called new activity, it might be one the participant has just learned about or one that person has been doing for some time but has recently come to view as of significantly greater importance than heretofore.

We may hypothesize that the deeper the fulfillment derived from the activity the greater the resistance to abandoning it. In this situation personal investment is high, rewards are numerous and powerfully attractive, and the enthusiast is motivated by, among other conditions, membership in an evolved social world, absorption in a leisure career and sense of an absorbing central life interest. There are costs, to be sure, but they must be highly disagreeable to lead someone to quit an activity holding such allure.

Social psychological contingencies

Here, in line with Contingency 3, the participant is, for social reasons, no longer able to participate, buffeted as this person is by such pressures as those stemming from work, family, or the irresistible appeal of another leisure activity. This is familiar territory for many a leisure studies specialist and, accordingly, there has been, albeit served up in different terminology, sporadic discussion of Antecedents three, four, and five (on work see Florida, 2014; on women's leisure and family, see Samuel, 1996, p. 2). I addressed myself to Contingency 3 in an exploration of the leisure lifestyle of mountain hobbyists in kayaking, snowboarding, and mountain climbing as these men and women strove to integrate the demands of work and family with their serious leisure passion (Stebbins, 2005a). Failure in this regard forced a small number of them to quit that passion for several years.

Contingency 4 is exemplified by a variety of social psychological pressures, among them chronic and intolerably intense stage fright, fierce inter-competitor rivalry and bitter relations with a leader such as a coach, director, or manager. Thus, Coakley (1992) found that adolescent elite athletes can 'burnout,' grow disenchanted with their sport because of intense competition, rigorous training and practice schedules and little opportunity to explore other aspects of life that might also foster personal development. Stand-up comic Andrew Smith stayed off the stage for years, gripped by a fear of 'bombing,' of failing to make the audience laugh (Borns, 1987, pp. 153–154). He sustained his interest in the art through writing scripts for films and sketches.

The following illustrate Contingency 5. The participant permanently loses a close friend or other partner who participated regularly with that person in the leisure activity in question, a situation that renders impossible continued involvement in it. Moreover, it occasionally happens that a local activity club disbands, leaving many former members with no outlet for the activity it formerly organized. And far too common in these times of budgetary restraint is the possibility that a municipality might close a needed recreational facility or program, leaving users with no local alternative.

Physical contingencies

Participants in this type are physically unable to continue further with an activity (Contingencies 6 and 7). Whereas abandonment in amateur, professional, and hobbyist sport for these reasons is fairly well documented, it is very much less so in other physically based leisure activities (for a review of abandonment in sport, see Waddington, 2000, pp. 414–419). These include music, dance, acrobatics, and the multitude of physically based hobbies (e.g., hunting, aerobics, woodworking, orienteering, needlecraft, mushroom collecting). For example, a newly acquired, enduring disability in a leg could eliminate weekend bird-watching as long-term numbness to a hand following a stroke could destroy a fulfillment career in knitting.[19]

The aging process also eventually forces many people, not all of them elderly, to renounce some favorite leisure activities (Contingency 8). We have already seen the effects of aging in elite-amateur and professional sport. Nonetheless, this process appears to be as potent outside as inside sport. Thus, arthritis in the fingers, a disease associated with aging in later life, can force leisure abandonment in elderly violinists, knitters, painters, and those with a passion for origami. Deteriorating eyesight can drive people from such hobbies as sewing, reading, lapidary work, and gun and bow-and-arrow marksmanship. Other components of Contingency 8 include diseases causing hearing impairment, weakness of hands and limbs, and increase in general fatigue, all of which can lead participants to terminate a variety of serious pursuits. Stebbins (1996a, pp. 58–59) briefly explored the effects of aging on participation in barbershop singing, and Midlarsky and Kahana (1994, p. 227) mention serious illness as one reason seniors in the 85-plus age category give for dropping out of volunteering.

Geographic contingencies

Leisure abandonment associated with one or more geographic contingencies (Contingency 9) has received precious little attention in the leisure studies literature. Examples of such contingencies include low water in rivers and lakes, lack of snow, insufficient ice (because of warm weather), absence of wind, too much rain or snow, and environmental pollution. These conditions, when linked as antecedents to geographic leisure abandonment, must be shown to block over a long period of time (e.g., several years) participation in a particular activity. Accordingly, such abandonment cannot be said to occur when a golf outing is canceled because of thundershowers or a snowstorm prevents people from reaching the ski slopes that day. A warm winter can preclude ice climbing for an entire season or a summer of heavy rain can wipe out the floral gardening scene. But neither one is a contingency, which is of such temporal magnitude that participants are inclined to permanently give up on the affected activity and look for a replacement.

Recent global climatic changes could, in theory, be engendering geographic leisure abandonment at what may be unprecedented rates in activities where technology has been insufficient to offset the changes. Perhaps, but I could find no research in this area, even while plausible examples exist. Thus, severe forest fires in western North America have probably eliminated local camping as well as certain kinds of berry picking (both are seasonal casual leisure activities). Further, years of drought in the same region appear to have eliminated trout fishing in some creeks whose water levels are now too low to support fish life.

Furthermore, geographic leisure abandonment can result from excessive use of an area by people and their institutions. For instance, the grizzly bear hunt in the Canadian Rockies appears to be on its way to extinction, in wake of governmental policy to issue fewer and fewer annual hunting licenses as a way of heading off the bears' own extinction. The annual hunt combined with highway kill, railroad deaths, and human exploitation and encroachment on their habitat by way of back packing and day hiking are exacting their toll. Historically, numerous species of bird, fish, reptile, and animal have, for the same reasons, met with extinction or near-extinction, not only in North America but also in some other regions of the world (e.g., the elephant in Africa; see Leakey & Morell, 2001). And how often has industrial pollution in almost every corner of the planet eliminated for the long term such casual and serious leisure as swimming and sport fishing (e.g., river pollution in China, *The Economist*, 2004)?

Regulatory contingencies

A regulatory contingency emerges when would-be participants are barred by a governing authority from entering a particular activity (Contingency 10). Thus, in many organized amateur and hobbyist athletic, artistic, and scientific endeavors, age or number of years of 'eligibility', if not both, help determine who participates in, for example, junior sport (in Canada), youth orchestras, young writers' competitions, and adolescent science fairs. Volunteer service on a board of directors is often fixed at one or two terms. Along different lines, certain kinds of (usually illegal) deviant behavior such as rape, drug use (including use of performance-enhancing substances) and property offense often lead to expulsion from the team or list of individual competitors of the amateur or hobbyist activity in question (Contingency 11).

And, following on Contingency 12, leisure abandonment sometimes results from, for instance, losing a qualifying race or, more rarely probably, a race in the final competition. Such abandonment is especially common in elite-amateur sport, as observed in, for instance, the European, Commonwealth, and Olympic Games. Other examples include failing at tryouts to get selected for a sports team (in Canadian football, see Stebbins, 1993a, pp. 108–109); failing to win an audition leading to membership in a theater company, community orchestra or local dance group; failing to win jury approval to hang paintings at an exhibition; and rejection of a manuscript by a book or periodical editor. True, in many of these examples the participant rolls with the punch and soldiers on, refusing to abandon the leisure. But sometimes such failure comes as the crowning blow, prompting the person to quit the activity for one more likely to generate success.

Favoritism and discrimination also constitute a special kind of regulatory contingency (Contingency 13). I have interpreted this as regulatory, because the individual's statutory right to participation and fair evaluation have been violated. That is, favoritism and discrimination are according to the rules forbidden, but nonetheless occur. It does happen that, for instance, a player is told in mid-season by the coach that he or she will no longer play a certain position, forcing the first to abandon that sport (this assumes no other outlet for it exists). It is possible, or might be alleged, that the coach's decision was based on discrimination or favoritism, as opposed to objective judgment of the quality of the player's performance.

Drift toward leisure abandonment

Discussion to this point might lead one to believe that leisure abandonment is a phenomenon we are always aware of; that is, facing a certain contingency people consciously decide to quit an activity. And abandonment motivated by Contingencies 5–7 and 9–13 gives considerable weight to this impression. But *drift*, a process we are usually much less conscious of, describes well the circumstances leading to leisure abandonment that does not necessarily presume a conscious decision to quit an activity. It is the third alternative for exiting a leisure activity.

Consider a couple of hypothetical examples. A musician in the local civic orchestra has been growing ever more disenchanted with the drift of the group's concert material toward popular music and show tunes, a trend arising from a financial need to increase the size of its paying audiences. One day, while comparing the attractiveness of today's concerts with that of past concerts, our musician realizes the great fulfillment once experienced in public orchestral performance has become significantly diluted (Contingency 1). Now it is clear that the time has come to formally sever ties with the group. In another example, pressure at work (Contingency 3) as felt, let us say, through a major increase in hours of employment, leads some workers to participate less and less in a particular leisure activity, even while never formally deciding to abandon it. She simply takes up her knitting needles less often, and he simply goes to his metalworking shop less frequently. Perhaps in the latter case, conscious abandonment happens only when the hobbyist decides to sell his tools.

Conclusions

Although the negative contingencies can appear at any stage of the fulfillment career, it may well be that leisure abandonment is somewhat more likely to occur during the career's beginning, development, and decline stages. It is because commitment to the career is most tenuous during these periods. Beginning and development, in particular, can be filled with frustration, self-doubt, competing free-time interests, and more. By late establishment and throughout maintenance, however, such sentiments and conditions have for the most part been dealt with. There is no need anymore to leave the activity for these reasons. With decline, if it sets in at all, abandonment may emerge as a way of adjustment to an activity that has become dispiritingly less rewarding than it once was.

The possibility of abandoning an activity applies to all the serious pursuits. We will therefore revisit the matter at several points in the remaining chapters of this book.

4
Finding Fulfillment in a Hobby

In this chapter, we will follow much the same road map as in Chapter 3, though now with interest centered on the five types of hobbies and their subtypes. The main interest here is, as it was earlier, to examine the nature of the first three stages of the fulfillment career in collecting, making and tinkering, noncompetitive participatory activities, sports and games (without professional counterparts), and the liberal arts hobbies. As we have done earlier, here also we will consider careers in each type as they are shaped by the six distinguishing qualities and the various costs and rewards. Similarly, maintenance and decline will, for the most part, be taken up later in Chapter 7, which deals mainly with the kinds of devotee work that can follow from these hobbies.

Early careers in collecting

Collecting as a hobby is a type of leisure in which a person purposely and systematically acquires particular objects of aesthetic, historical, scientific, or other value fired by the goal of completing the collection. Collectors determine what their completed collection will consist of, such as all coins minted in the United States between 1900 and 1950, all coins minted throughout the world during that period, or all coins minted in Britain across its history. Most collectors acquire objects that are also valued by some other people, including those who collect those same objects. Nevertheless, people exist who are motivated to collect objects valued only by themselves and, perhaps, a few others; for example, pine cones or waste baskets.

The range and diversity of collectibles is enormous, as seen in stamps, paintings, rare books, violins, minerals, and butterflies. With experience collectors become more knowledgeable about the social, commercial, and physical circumstances in which they acquire their cherished items. They also develop a sophisticated appreciation of these items, consisting in part of a broad understanding of their historical and contemporary use, production, and significance.

Compared with commercial dealers (see Chapter 7) hobbyist collectors are clearly a different breed. The dealers acquire their stock to make a living from its subsequent sales; their motives diverge sharply from those driving the hobbyist collectors. Although the latter may try to make enough money selling a violin or painting to buy one of greater value, they are usually more interested in gaining a prestigious item for social and personal reasons, or possibly for hedging inflation, than in contributing directly to their livelihood. Additionally, unlike the typical dealer many collectors hope to acquire an entire series or category of a collectible (e.g., all the posters of the Newport Jazz Festival, all the books in the Nancy Drew series).

The casual collecting of such things as rocks, pins, and beer bottles is, at best, marginal hobbyism. With such items, there is nowhere near the equivalent complexity of social, commercial, and physical circumstances to learn about; scant substantial aesthetic or technical appreciation to be cultivated; no comparable level of understanding of production and use to be developed. Casual collecting is therefore most accurately classified as casual leisure, as simple diversion. As Allan Olmsted (1991) once put it, those who collect with little seriousness are 'accumulators'. Nor does the hobby of collecting encompass those who hoard, say, canned goods or gasoline, which are practical acquisitions for the future.

The variety of hobbyist collections pursued today is huge. Fortunately, Robert Overs (1984) brought some order to this chaos some time ago by developing a ninefold classification of collections. I use his scheme here, though with several modifications and additions needed to bring it in line with our definition of hobbyist activity.

- Poster collections
- Coin, currency, medal collections
- Stamp collections

- Collections of natural objects (fossils; animal trophies and stuffed specimens; moths, insects, and butterflies; ferns and wild flowers; leaves, pine cones, and other arboreal objects; rocks, stones, and minerals; pearls, seashells, starfish, sponges, and other oceanic objects)[1]
- Model collections (e.g., trains, cars, ships)
- Doll collections
- Collections of art objects (e.g., plates, books, CDs/records, figurines, paintings, sculptures, musical instruments)
- Antique collections (e.g., toys, cars, books, clocks, bottles, furniture)
- Contemporary popular culture collections (e.g., pins, comics, sports cards, baseball caps, pop CDs/records)

The beginning

Merely accumulating coins or stamps without hobbyist intentions may be classified as a kind of dabbling, leading possibly to serious collecting of these objects. But some accumulation, say, of subscription magazines or foreign currency may be for practical reasons: need to consult back issues or use the currency for future travel. In any case, we have seen that dabbling is not a necessary precursor to the serious pursuits.

The process that spurs on many people to become neophytes in collecting is their initial 'interaction' with the object of their affection: the collectible coin, doll, seashell, sports card, and so on. Some people are taken with the beauty of the object (e.g., stamp collectors, Gelber, 1992). For others, its appeal lies in its sociocultural and historical contexts, as is true for collectors of posters, baseball caps, Civil War guns, and musical instruments. The would-be collector knows something about these contexts and is drawn to the object in part because of this knowledge. There may also be an aesthetic attraction here. A third axis of object interaction treats the collectible as a souvenir. Thus, a tourist buys a figurine representative of a certain part of the world or a concert-goer buys a poster of a concert just attended. Enamored of such purchases, these (now) neophyte collectors decide to expand their collection, say, by searching gift and antique shops for regional figurines or art and bookstores for posters commemorating similar concerts in the past.

That some people see certain objects worth collecting as invest-ments clouds the hobbyist nature of the activity. When pins, stamps, comics, sports cards, and baseball caps, for example, are regarded in this light, the purely leisure motive of engaging in the activity is diluted for this kind of collector, sometimes substantially. Neverthe-less, it is possible to have both a leisure and an economic interest in a collectible, such as to appreciate its sociocultural/historical context along with its investment potential.

Preparation time is short for the collector compared with, for example, that of the amateur. Having made the decision to collect, neophytes need only determine where to go and what to look for. Still, since some things are not worth collecting, they must study in advance the criteria used to identify collectible fossils, glass sculp-ture, or oil paintings. Collectors of natural objects will find that they need instruction on how to preserve what they find. Storage of col-lected items can also be fraught with problems, which a seasoned collector has learned to solve. For instance, a dry environment can cause antique furniture to crack and bookbindings to putrefy. Only accumulators collect with no preparation whatsoever.

Eventually collectors make a conscious decision to collect, leading thereby to becoming a neophyte. Yet, some may drift toward this sta-tus, acquiring haphazardly, for example, two or three objects before deciding to make collecting a proper hobby. This turning point is crit-ical for several reasons. First, the costs of collecting the object must now be considered. Second, since a collection is supposed to expand, where will it be housed? Stamps and coins pose storage problems different from those posed by old cars and jukeboxes. Third, people living with the collector may weigh in on the effects of the collec-tion on their domestic and, perhaps, financial lives. Considerations of this nature may, when sufficiently problematic, obviate becoming a neophyte in this hobby.

Beginning collectors have their work cut out for them. They must learn where to find their collectibles, be this online, in special-ized shops, in private homes, through collectors clubs, along certain sections of beach or forest, and on and on. Moreover, collections must be cataloged, preserved, and those of significant value secured. And collectors must learn how to spot forgeries, fakes, and dis-honest dealers and sellers, problems that Olmsted (1988, p. 279) says plague most areas of collecting, particularly when the objects collected have material value. Leisure careers in the collecting hobbies revolve heavily around acquisition, on acquiring objects and knowledge about them. As the collector gains more of both, this person's career advances, refracted from time to time in new directions by different contingencies and turning points encountered along the way.

Development

In the development stage, collectors bring such challenges under control, typically through a combination of experience, advice from other collectors (e.g., face-to-face, print and online media, members of a local club or national organization), and common sense. This is also the period during which collectors physically situate their collections, depending on size of object collected, resulting in many cases in a combined office and storehouse. Here, with the collectibles at hand, they can be cataloged, preserved, and secured and, of course, repeatedly beheld for their beauty and significance.

Later on in development, some collectors (e.g., of coins, stamps, dolls) participate in shows or museum exhibitions expressly organized for displaying to the larger public the featured items. Moreover, samples of these items may be conveniently, if not conspicuously, displayed for the pleasure of visitors to the collector's home. These activities and others give substance to the hobby, and invite the collector to expand the amount of time, and possibly money, devoted to it.

Establishment

During this stage, collecting finds its rhythm in daily life. Here some types of collectors get into the habit of haunting the auctions, garage sales, antique shops, flea markets, and used book and record stores. And their social worlds may be further constituted of one or more commercial dealers of the items they are searching for. Patronage of their shops and Web sites can become routine.

In establishment, the hobby may come to consume so much of a person's free time that friends and relatives start to wonder whether the 'passion' has got out of hand. Whether passionate collectors are mentally disturbed, as some writers maintain, or only engulfed by the deep self-fulfillment that can come from such serious leisure, or both, is a question that has long fascinated both experts and lay people (Belk, 2004, p. 197). By exploiting the participant's relevant natural tastes and talents, serious leisure activities do help realize individual human potential. The desire for more experience of this sort is infectious, which might appear to some as a sign of psychological disorder.

Whereas some kinds of collecting are clearly for the rich (e.g., fine paintings, rare violins, antique cars), this hobby is, in general, accessible to all ages, ethnic categories, and social classes. Still space and security may be problems for some people, even when they aspire to collect objects as small as stamps or bottle caps. But, from a financial standpoint, note that many collectibles are freely available, among them, leaves, rocks, insects, and sea shells, or moderately priced, for example, sports cards, comic books, and baseball caps.

The collector's social world

In many of the collecting hobbies, the corresponding social worlds are anchored in a local club or national organization, sometimes both. Although collecting itself is an individual activity, the clubs provide members with a place for showing kindred enthusiasts the items they have collected and garnering insider information about how to acquire the best specimens of their kind of collectible. Some collectors are aided in their search by dealers (e.g., in art, stamps, coins), who make up another part of the core of the social world of the first. Meanwhile, the clubs take on a special importance for many of the dealers, who use them as outlets for displaying their wares and advertising their services.

The social worlds of some collectors are further made up of the people and establishments they must deal with to obtain the items they are searching for. Apart from patronizing the dealers, who are usually expensive, stamp collectors often develop sets of contacts – friends, acquaintances, relatives – who bring them stamps from time to time. On seeing a pin they like, collectors in this field approach its wearer in hope of trading a pin for the one desired. Antique collectors eventually hear about the shops most likely to carry items of interest to them, after which they set about perfecting the art of haggling with the staff in hope of buying at the best price. They as well as some other kinds of collectors also get into the habit of haunting the auctions, garage sales, and flea markets. Some collectible items such as guns and stamps are presented periodically at shows. It is also true, however, that many collections are not at all social as just described. To pursue these hobbies, these collectors need only head for the woods or the shore or curl up on the couch with a good mail-order or online catalog.

Early careers in making and tinkering

Grouped under this heading are such enthusiasts as inventors, seamstresses, automobile repairers, and toy and furniture makers. Excluded from it are the do-it-yourself drudges who, to avoid the expense of a full-time tradesperson, for instance, paint the exterior of their houses. Their motives contrast sharply with those of the hobbyist home remodeler, repairer, and handyman. The fulfillment careers leading from this set of hobbies into devotee work make a complicated subject. It will be explored in Chapter 7.

Although it may seem odd, it is entirely consistent with the extended meaning of the 'maker' part of this category to include within it those hobbyists who breed or display fish, birds, reptiles, and animals. This same heading also embraces the people who avocationally breed or display such animals as dogs, cats, sheep, horses, ferrets, and, in recent years in the mountainous areas of western North America, llamas. We return to these raisers and breeders later in this section.

Robert Overs' (1984) classification of 'craft activities' provides some of the framework for the following discussion of the making and tinkering hobbies. A somewhat more detailed description of each is available elsewhere (Stebbins, 2013c, pp. 68–75).

- Cooking, baking, and candy-kaking
- Beverage crafts
- Decorating activities (arranging flowers, decorating small objects)
- Interlacing, interlocking, and knot-making activities (including fly-tying)
- Toy, model, and kit assembly
- Paper crafts (including bookbinding, scrapbook projects, and papier-mâché constructions)
- Leather and textile crafts (this includes sewing and quilting)
- Wood and metalworking activities (including whittling)
- Handyman activities (see below)

- Raising and breeding (including gardening)
- Miscellaneous crafts (see below)

Earlier I mentioned the do-it-yourself drudge. Still, some people find some do-it-yourself projects to be quite agreeable, to be project-based leisure as described in Chapter 1. Scattered single do-it-yourself projects do not, however, amount to a hobby. But keeping in good running order one's own home and perhaps the homes of friends, relatives, and neighbors can turn into a regular and most worthwhile pursuit. Such a pursuit – that of the handyman – requires an immense range of skills and knowledge applied to appliance repair, plumbing work, electrical work, and interior and exterior house construction and decoration. The last of these requires proficiency with tile, paint, varnish, siding, panels, roofing, drywall, and wallpaper to mention some of the more common materials. Auto and small engine repair is also part of this list, again with the proviso that it be done regularly and primarily for leisure fulfillment. That hobbyists here occasionally save themselves money by avoiding commercial services in no way comprises their more fundamental serious leisure motive of seeking deeply rewarding activity for its own sake. And, speaking of commercial services, handyman businesses operate in many cities (see Chapter 7).

Among the miscellaneous crafts are making candles and creating mosaics from such materials as glass, paper, and marble. Furthermore, many adults and children find great fulfillment both in kite making and then in flying their constructions in a nearby field. Lapidary work – the art of cutting and polishing stones – is another miscellaneous craft. And then there are those who have a passion for making interesting objects with beads, buttons, or plaster or by way of the art of glass blowing. Finally, the hobby of perfume making holds a unique allure for its enthusiasts.

The beginning and development

Many of the crafts depend for their deepest fulfillment on the development of substantial, specialized skills, as seen in using a knife to whittle, a needle to sew, or a plane to make furniture. Other crafts, when pursued at their most rewarding levels, require considerable background knowledge. Cooking, do-it-yourself, and raising and breeding exemplify well this prerequisite. Thus, Baldwin and Norris (1999) observed that dog enthusiasts commonly enrolled in a dog training class, where they discovered that they had a talent for working with their dog and owned a particularly fine specimen of its breed. Furthermore, hobbyists who assemble toys, models, and other objects from kits, like those who sew from patterns and cook from recipes, must have a talent for following often complicated instructions and paying attention to detail. Those in the woodworking and metalworking fields along with some of the hobbyist do-it-yourselfers must also develop a capacity for creating their own plans and designs. Lastly, some of these activities can be most artistic, as is evident in working with rocks, making mosaics, and decorating certain objects.

This is the stuff of the hobbyist career, which participants sense as they improve in skill, knowledge, artistry, attention to detail, or a combination of these. In this sense, careers in the making and tinkering hobbies resemble those in the amateur fields. But there are certain construction hobbies with comparatively light developmental requirements that revolve primarily around the accumulation of completed projects. These include some of the projects discussed under the headings of paper crafts, miscellaneous crafts, and interlacing and interlocking activities.

Dabbling is uncommon in these hobbies, it being limited primarily to whittling, scrapbooking, and certain kinds of decorating. In general, then, participants must enter as neophytes, with an eye to acquiring the rudimentary skills and knowledge needed to engage even superficially in the activity. Although adult education courses are routinely offered on nearly all the making and tinkering hobbies, self-directed learning about them from books, magazine articles, and online sources may be at least as popular. The initial impetus prodding someone into beginning a fulfillment career in one of these hobbies is probably as varied as the hobbies themselves. As with all the other serious pursuits, the beginner must be able to identify strongly with the core activities of the hobby.

Establishment

In establishment the makers and tinkerers hit their stride. For some this means a regular, or reasonably regular, schedule of making their specialty in their workshop. Nonetheless, handymen cannot usually be so regular; they must wait for worthwhile projects to appear (e.g., the stove breaks down, house needs painting, new desk must be assembled). Hobbyist cooks and bakers commonly must wait for occasions consistent with their specialty such as holiday celebrations, dinner parties, and nonwork days with enough time to prepare a gourmet dish or meal. Raising and breeding animals and plants requires this type of maker to meet their needs.

For some makers and tinkerers, being established includes regular participation in expositions of their products. And some of these may be competitive, as when juried prizes are awarded. At certain expositions and outside them at events designed for sales, some makers occasionally or routinely try to sell their products. Bake sales, often intended to aid a charity, are an example. Elsewhere, pursuing the paper, interlacing, textile, metal, and woodworking crafts may also result in products that may be sold or donated.

In fact, a common problem in this area for many established participants is how to dispose of what they have made. Some makers run out of room to store their products. Others want people to use or enjoy what they have made (while storage space may also be problematic). They may try to sell some of their products or they may concentrate on giving them away. The gifts could be to friends and relatives or to a charitable cause (e.g., knit goods to the needy, decorated objects to a hospital or home for the elderly).[2] Cooks, bakers, candy confectioners, along with brewers and vintners seem largely immune to this problem, since typically, they or someone else soon consumes (or, if unpalatable, throws out) what they produce.

Social world

The social worlds associated with the different making and tinkering pastimes are equally varied, offering something for nearly everyone. Many of these activities allow participants to work alone, becoming socially linked with others only to the extent necessary to get supplies for making their products and the extent needed to display them once completed. Hobbyists preferring greater social involvement can usually find a club to join. Or they may hang around the local shops that serve hobbyists with like interests, chatting with clerks and customers. Some makers and tinkerers take advantage of the occasional noncredit course offered in their area. And in many of these hobbies, the aforementioned fairs and expositions (held annually, semiannually, sporadically) give them the opportunity to display their own work as well as view that of kindred enthusiasts. Furthermore, since many makers and tinkerers provide their products or services free of charge, often as gifts, they gain direct contact with a small number of outsiders. These outsiders are also part of the participants' social world.

Noncompetitive participatory activities

In activity participation, the hobbyist steadfastly does a kind of leisure that requires systematic physical movement, has inherent appeal, and is pursued within a set of rules. Often the activity poses a challenge (usually one provided by nature), where inter-human competition, if there is any, is not an essential part of it. When carried out continually for these reasons, the activities included in this type are as diverse as fishing, video games, and barbershop singing.[3] The two types of activity participation on which at least some career-related data exist are discussed here as nature activities and body-centered activities.

Nature activities

This extremely diverse set of interests is pursued in the outdoors. Sorted here into the categories of nature appreciation, nature challenge, and nature exploitation, most are enjoyed most of the time away from towns and cities. Still, within the natural areas in the towns and cities, we may be able to fish, watch birds, cross-country ski, and fly model airplanes, to mention a few possibilities.

Nature appreciation

At the center of the nature appreciation activities lies the awe-inspiring natural environment in which they take place. Seeing, hearing, smelling, and feeling the surroundings – 'getting out in nature' – add up to a powerful reason for doing one or more of the following:

- hiking;
- horse riding;
- back packing/wilderness camping;
- spelunking (cave exploration);[4]
- bird-watching;

- canoeing/kayaking;
- SCUBA diving/snorkeling;
- snowshoeing;
- snowmobiling.

Another important reason for pursuing these activities is to learn and express the skills and knowledge needed to find fulfillment in them. At this level, they are serious leisure (Davidson & Stebbins, 2011). Moreover, some can pose a substantial natural challenge, discussed below as white-water canoeing and back-country snowshoeing.

Nature's challenges

A nature challenge activity (NCA) is a leisure pursuit whose core activity or activities center on meeting a test posed by the surrounding natural environment. As pointed out elsewhere, considerable nature appreciation is also possible in these activities, though at times the challenges are so stiff that they concentrate the mind more or less exclusively on trying to meet them (Davidson & Stebbins, 2011). These activities include:

- ballooning;
- flying;
- gliding;
- wave surfing;
- alpine skiing;
- snowboarding;
- SCUBA diving;
- cross-country skiing;
- sailing (with sail/engine);
- parachuting and skydiving;
- hang gliding;
- mountain climbing;
- back-country snowshoeing;
- white water canoeing and kayaking; and
- dirt (trail) bike, jeep, quad runner riding (noncompetitive).

Thus, an accomplished cross-country skier can savor the beauty of the snow-covered trees and partially frozen streams near trails set on moderate terrain. But, then, a steep descent with a sharp turn in the middle suddenly diverts all attention to skiing technique.

Nature exploitation

In these hobbies, if all goes well, participants come away from their sessions in nature with some of its 'yield', as experienced in fishing, hunting, trapping, and mushroom gathering. Yet, the fishers, the hunters, and the rest do appreciate nature as well, though not when they have a fish on the line or a deer in their sights. Such situations concentrate awareness on the core activity.

Body-centered hobbies

The body-centered hobbies draw the participant's attention directly to his or her body. This is in contrast to the nature activities where one's attention is fixed on one or more captivating aspects of nature. In the nature activities, the body is a vehicle with which to appreciate or exploit nature or meet one of its many challenges.[5] By contrast, routine exercise is a body-centered hobby, though only to the extent that it involves skill and knowledge and is considered fulfilling. Swimming, bodybuilding, ice skating, roller skating, running, and the martial arts when used for conditioning number among the exercise activities qualifying as serious leisure.

Gymnastics, tumbling, and acrobatics fall into a separate category of body-centered hobbies. Although they obviously offer a good deal of exercise, the goal of perfecting a set of difficult bodily maneuvers, or 'feats', is equally important. The same may be said for another corporeal activity: ballroom dancing. It, too, provides exercise, while inspiring its enthusiasts to master such dances as the waltz, foxtrot, samba, rumba, and tango.[6]

Starting out

Dabbling is possible in several nature appreciation activities, among them, hiking, spelunking, bird-watching, canoeing, snowshoeing, and snowmobiling. Rosenbaum (2013, p. 647) found that most jeepers stumbled on to their hobbyist careers through casual participation in a friend's off-road excursion or a corporate-sponsored event. Indeed, it appears that, as hobbies, most people get started by initially dabbling in them, although those curious about canoeing or snowshoeing, for instance, usually first have to rent or borrow the needed equipment.[7] By contrast, the NCAs, before they may be pursued, require some preliminary instruction and, depending on the activity, special equipment and services. The same holds for the nature exploitation activities.

Neophytes, in this case those who have a commitment to learning the rudiments of their participatory activity, are inspired by the dream that once they have mastered them they could experience some significant rewards. Learning enough of the basics to gain this sense of the activity's potential for self-fulfillment may be achieved formally or informally, if not by both routes. Adult education courses of varying lengths exist for all these activities, while some also lend themselves to informal instruction. Hiking, backpacking, canoeing, fishing, hunting, and mushrooming number among the participatory activities often effectively learned on the spot from seasoned relatives or friends.

Development and establishment

All the participation activities, when undertaken as serious leisure, call for a significant amount of physical conditioning. A career in this kind of leisure depends on it. Even those who sail, hunt, hike, or watch birds must be fit enough to pursue these interests for at least a couple of hours. Still, some of these activities are less demanding than others. So, hang-gliding and fishing from a boat require low levels of conditioning compared with such activities as swimming, gymnastics, and cross-country skiing where considerable conditioning is necessary. Nonetheless, age aside, the many rewards of activity participation as a major type of serious leisure await all who want to be physically active.

As with the making and tinkering hobbies, careers in the activity participation hobbies further unfold along certain distinctive dimensions, two of which are skill and stamina. Both are salient in pursuits like tumbling, wave surfing, roller skating, mountain climbing, cross-country skiing, and ballroom dancing.[8] And, as development shades to establishment, the number of projects completed becomes an important dimension for some of these hobbyists, as seen in their lists of important caves explored, notable mountains climbed, or major rivers canoed.[9] The accumulation of knowledge and experience is a prominent fourth dimension in the nature exploitation hobbies.

As an example, consider the fishing hobbies with their rich lore of baits, weather conditions, and feeding habits as it relates to angling for different species of fish. These dimensions form the foundation on which these hobbyists build their personal and social identities.[10]

Establishment in a participatory activity brings with it extensive involvement in its unique social world. With the exceptions of ballroom dancing and team sailing, literally every such activity can be pursued alone by people with a taste for solitude. Indeed, many of them can only be pursued alone. Others, among them canoeing, spelunking, backpacking, and hunting, are commonly done with someone else, if for no other reason than the help and security a partner might provide during emergencies. Whether pursued alone or with others, most participation hobbies have local clubs whose goals include organizing collective outings, serving as repositories of useful information about equipment and nearby sites for pursuing the activity, and holding get-togethers where members can talk shop to their heart's content. Another institution in the social world of some activity participants is the equipment dealer and repair service – the sporting goods store, the backcountry supplier, the wilderness outfitter. Others find their leisure lives organized around certain gyms, pools, rinks, and dance floors. In activity participation, as in so many other forms of serious leisure, the social world of any particular physical activity is encompassing enough to foster a lifestyle in its own right.

Competitive sports and games

The chief difference separating competitors from activity participants is the presence of the most essential component of any sport or game: interpersonal competition. Both types of hobby are organized according to sets of rules but, in the sports, games, and contests, these rules are always set out in formal terms – in rule books, on printed sheets – designed to control competitive action in (usually) numerous specific ways. The sports are presented here according to their classification as team or individual. Descriptions of each can be found in the larger encyclopedias.

Team sports

- Polo
- Curling

- Lacrosse
- Ringette
- Doubles versions of individual sports (e.g., handball, table tennis)

Individual sports

- Darts
- Horseshoes
- Shuffleboard
- Pool/billiards/snooker
- Croquet
- Handball (singles)
- Race walking
- Long-distance running
- Target, trap, and skeet shooting
- Table tennis (ping-pong)
- Orienteering
- Martial arts (e.g., jujitsu, karate, aikido, tae kwon do)
- Dog and sled-dog racing
- Iceboat racing
- Powerboat racing
- Model racing (e.g., boats, cars, trains, airplanes)

Orienteering, a sport of Norwegian origin, is a cross-country race on foot guided by map and compass. Ringette (Ringette/Ringuette Canada, 2012) is a kind of ice hockey in which a rubber ring is used instead of a puck. Invented in Canada and now played internationally, it is primarily a sport for females. Race walking, executed with a special rolling, stiff-legged gait, is distinguished from power walking (exercise) and strolling (casual leisure).

Games, puzzles, and mazes

Although the terms 'sport' and 'game' are frequently used interchangeably in commonsense, for our purposes we must differentiate them. A sport is a game based on one or more physical skills, whereas as such skills have no place in other games. Further, chance figures heavily in many nonsport games, seen in drawing cards, shaking dice, spinning dials and wheels, and so on. Granted, there are also chance elements in sport games, but they are not an inherent part of the game. In this sense, the nonsport games of chess and checkers resemble sport games.

Since they can never qualify as serious leisure, games based purely on chance (e.g., craps, bingo, roulette) are omitted from the following list. To qualify as serious leisure, an activity must make use of developed skills, knowledge, experience, or a combination of these three. A game can have chance components and still become a hobby, however, because it also allows decision-making informed by accumulated knowledge of and experience with the game.

Table and board games

- Dual combat games (e.g., Chess, Checkers, Backgammon)
- Money games (e.g., Rich Uncle, Monopoly)
- Playing piece games (e.g., Sorry, Parcheesi, Chinese checkers)
- Racing games (e.g., Snakes and Ladders)

Card and dice games

- Card games for one or two people (e.g., cribbage, gin rummy, the solitaires)
- Card games for three or more playing as individuals (e.g., hearts, poker, rummy, black jack, canasta)
- Card games for three or more playing as a team (e.g., bridge, whist, sheep's head, pinochle)[11]
- Craps (dice)

Knowledge and word games

- Scrabble, charades, Pictionary, Trivial Pursuit, among others
- Quizzes

Electronic games

- Computer games (video-console games now available on computers)
- Video-console games

Role-playing games

- Chivalry and Sorcery
- Dungeons and Dragons

- Empire of the Petal Throne
- Traveller

Miscellaneous games

- Backgammon
- Dominoes

Because they are noncompetitive, the puzzles and mazes designed for leisure purposes are not games in the strictest sense of the definition just set out. More accurately, puzzles and mazes are diversions designed to test the ingenuity, knowledge, or insight of the player. The crossword, acrostic, jigsaw, and mechanical puzzles (e.g., Rubik's Cube) are popular, as are the 'brain twisters' like hidden pictures, memory tests, and the mathematical and logical puzzles. With the possible exception of the role-playing games, the games listed here need no introduction. Gary Fine (1983, p. 6) describes the role-playing, or fantasy, game is 'any game which allows a number of players to assume the roles of imaginary characters and operate with some degree of freedom in an imaginary environment'.

Careers

Strictly speaking, none of these sports and games can be dabbled in, for to truly play them requires at minimum knowledge of their basic rules (long-distance running is an exception). That is, when not guided by the rules, merely throwing a dart, shooting a pool ball, or pushing a shuffleboard puck, for instance, cannot be conceived of as dabbling in that sport. Beginners here are therefore always neophytes who have to learn the rules and who, in the case of sports enthusiasts, must also learn some elementary skills before they can participate on the most rudimentary level.

The observations made earlier about physical conditioning and age limitations for activity participants apply with equal validity to the sports mentioned in this section. Furthermore, the sports competitors also have leisure careers similar to those of the activity participants. On the other hand, people who play games have career patterns similar to those of some of the collectors and makers and tinkerers. With experience, they grow wiser and more sophisticated at playing a particular game (on this process in chess, see Puddephatt, 2005). In addition, puzzle solvers accumulate conquests; they solve

a growing number of puzzles, possibly moving up a scale of difficulty as their careers unfold to the point where they enter one of
the national or international puzzle contests. As long as the participant's mental acuity holds up, there is no age limit for the games
and puzzles, although deteriorating eyesight can certainly discourage
participating in them.

Social worlds

It is during establishment that the social worlds of the sports competitors and the players of games and solvers of puzzles evolve extensively. During this stage, the worlds of the sports competitors come to
resemble those of the activity participants. Thus, Major (2001) found
that competitive long-distance runners valued the 'social affiliation'
with other runners they experienced over their careers in the sport.

And the solitary players of games and solvers of puzzles share the
condition of aloneness with those activity participants who also cher-
ish it. Indeed, like the puzzle enthusiasts, many of the players going
in for solitaire and certain electronic games seem to pursue their
hobbies virtually alone, with little social contact of any kind. Furthermore, the social world of other games players is often minimal,
consisting only of those with whom they routinely play (e.g., the
wife and husband scrabble partners, Friday night poker group, and
Tuesday morning bridge players).

Still, clubs exist in some areas, notably bridge and the role-playing
games, and tournaments are now held in bridge, chess, scrabble, and
Monopoly. Absent from the social worlds of most games are the more
distant participants like critics, coaches, suppliers, service personnel,
and so on, people who enrich the social worlds of many other kinds
of serious leisure. Thus, by comparison, the social worlds of many of
the puzzlers and game players are simple, which, however, is not to
deny that many of them routinely find considerable fulfillment in
these hobbies.

The liberal arts hobbies

The liberal arts hobbyists are enamored of the systematic acquisition
of knowledge for its own sake. Many of them accomplish this by
reading voraciously in a field of art (fine and entertainment), sport,
cuisine, language, culture, history, science, philosophy, politics, or

belletristic fiction and poetry (Stebbins, 1994; 2013b, chapter 5).[12] But some of them go beyond this to expand their knowledge still further through cultural tourism, documentary videos, television programs, and similar resources. These hobbyists look on the knowledge and understanding they gain as an end in itself rather than, as is common in the other serious leisure pursuits, as background, as a means to fulfilling involvement in a hobby or an amateur activity. Compared with the other hobbies and the various amateur activities, the knowledge acquired in the liberal arts pastimes is of primary rather than secondary importance.

Though the matter has yet to be studied in detail, it is theoretically possible to separate buffs from consumers in the liberal arts hobbies of sport, cuisine, and the fine and entertainment arts. Some people – call them consumers – more or less uncritically consume restaurant fare, sports events, or displays of art (concerts, shows, exhibitions) as pure entertainment and sensory stimulation (casual leisure), whereas others – they are buffs – participate in these same situations as more or less knowledgeable experts, as serious leisure. The ever rarer Renaissance man of our day may also be classified here, even though such people avoid specializing in one field of learning. Instead, their goal is to acquire a somewhat more superficial knowledge of a variety of fields. Being broadly well read is thus a (liberal arts) hobby of its own.

The liberal arts hobbies are set off from the other serious leisure pursuits by two basic characteristics: the search for broad knowledge of an area of human life and the search for this information for its own sake. Broad knowledge may be compared with technical knowledge, an admittedly fuzzy distinction based on degree rather than on crisp boundaries. Still, we may say that unlike technical, or detailed, knowledge the broad kind is humanizing. Through it we can gain a deep understanding and acceptance of an important sector of human life (art, food, language, history, etc.) and the needs, values, desires, and sentiments found there. Nevertheless, this understanding and acceptance does not necessarily, or even usually, lead to adoption of the sector of life being studied.

Knowledge sought for its own sake implies that its practical application is secondary. Yet liberal arts hobbyists do use the broad knowledge they acquire. For instance, they find considerable satisfaction in expressing this knowledge, and the expression may be an important way for them to maintain and expand it. But this in no way relegates such knowledge to the status of a mere accessory, of being a simple means to a more highly valued end. That is how it often is in the other hobbies and in the amateur and volunteer fields. Here participants need certain kinds of practical information to produce anything of merit.

A third basic characteristic of the liberal arts hobby is the profundity of its broad knowledge; in other words, such knowledge is much more than merely entertaining. This characteristic, which is also found in the more technical bodies of knowledge associated with the other forms of serious leisure, is particularly relevant for the current politics hobbyist. While searching for profound news analyses, this hobbyist must constantly work to avoid or at least bracket what Altheide and Snow (1991, chapter 2; see also Stebbins, 2013b, p. 92) now refer to as the primarily entertaining and therefore rarely enlightening broadcasts and analyses of the political news heard on radio and television and seen on the Internet. Entertaining but uninformative mass media reports and analyses also torment liberal arts hobbyists in the areas of art, sport, and science. Yet, the unfortunate lot of many of these enthusiasts is that they often have little choice but to rely on these media for information.

Career: Beginning

What people do in the liberal arts hobbies has been labeled 'fulfilling reading' (Stebbins, 2013b, pp. ix–x). In contrast, 'pleasurable reading' of, for example, popular novels and articles is casual leisure. By definition, it fails to generate a leisure career. A third kind of reading – 'utilitarian reading' – is that done to acquire information of a profound nature (e.g., scholarly reading, some liberal arts reading). Fulfilling reading, which is often centered on a genre of literature, is commonly undertaken for inspiration, personal development, education, or a combination of these. Examples include reading studies and writings of a purely literary character, mainly essays, criticism as well as fine-art poetry, plays, stories, and novels.

The liberal arts hobbies offer an exceptionally flexible type of serious leisure. They can be carried out at the convenience of the person, molded around other activities (obligatory or not), and accommodated to the demands of work and family (Stebbins, 2013b, pp. 99–106). Scheduled courses, lectures, and radio and television programs sometimes momentarily undermine this flexibility. Still, with reading as the main activity, the hobbyist reader's leisure lifestyle is for these reasons unlikely to become too programmed.

Although advanced reading requires a variety of skills, people with an ordinary ability in this activity, as acquired in school or through self-directed learning, can easily dabble in the liberal arts fields.[13] Some children and adults, though unaccustomed to reading for pleasure, nonetheless get inspired to do just that after having, for example, seen publicity for a book, had a friend or relative recommend it, or observed someone reading it. In some cases, this initial experience turns out to be agreeable enough to want to repeat it with another book. By way of this growing interest, dabbling evolves into the beginning stage of a career as a liberal arts hobbyist, and as such, a committed reader. And, note that the material read need not be books, but may be articles, essays, short stories, pieces of poetry, among others.

Career: Development

Development in the liberal arts hobbies occurs primarily along two lines: reading skills and reading materials. Francine Prose (2009, pp. 86–91), in describing how to be a good writer, emphasizes the a priori requirement of being able to read well. She says:

> I read for pleasure, first, but also most analytically, conscious of style, of diction, of how sentences were formed and information was being conveyed, how the writer was structuring a plot, creating characters, employing detail and dialogue. And as I wrote I discovered that writing, like reading, was done one word at a time, one punctuation mark at a time.

Reading in this careful way is accomplished not only word by word, but also sentence by sentence, paragraph by paragraph, and so on as the reader ponders why the writer has chosen the words used, formed the sentences as they appear on the printed page, paragraphed entire passages, and, in general, structured the text (book, article, poem, etc.) as this person did. Prose also concentrates on the narration of the story, its various characters, and the dialog among them. In all this, the committed reader occasionally considers how the text might be improved a bit or at least differently created, as in using alternative words, sentences, paragraphing, narratives, and the like.

To be sure, there is more to the skill of reading than this dissecting of text. In novels and short stories, there are plots to be analyzed and, if appreciably imaginative, to be admired for their originality. Good writing makes liberal use of alliteration, metaphor, hyperbole, simile, and other figures of speech intended to vividly and imaginatively communicate meaning. Careful readers will also notice these creations, marvel if warranted at their effectiveness and imaginativeness, and possibly, as a playful aside, even take a turn at supplying some of their own.

Much of what has just been said also applies to reading skillfully essays, other nonfiction, utilitarian writing, and even some scientific tracts. Here, too, choice of words, structure of sentences, paragraphing, and lay out of the overall work are of utmost importance. There are no plots, but the absorbing use of figures of speech is always welcome.

The essays and utilitarian texts differ in required reading skills from fictional reading in that, for the first to be considered worthwhile, they must meet scholarly standards. In other words, there must be adequate evidence for all claims put forth, the logic of the argument must be easily apparent, the work must be grounded in the literature of the relevant fields bearing on the subject of the text, and so on. Skilled readers of such material, using these criteria, will know how to evaluate it.

In sum, the skills of reading fall into two great categories: artistic and analytic. Appreciation of the choice of words, structure of paragraphs, imaginativeness of plot, figures of speech, and so on comprise the artistic side of reading (and writing), whereas readers become analytic when they weigh evidence, consider the logic of an argument, and assess how well the work relates to the literature and similar interests. Criticism of literary works is an analytic undertaking. Utilitarian and fulfilling reading draw on one or both of these sets of skills, while reading for pleasure may be, and indeed often is, done without invoking significant capability in either.

Reading materials

The second main element of development in the liberal arts pursuits is locating the hobbyist reading material. Pleasurable reading has a strong commercial base, so books and magazines of this sort are easily and widely available. By comparison scholarly and belletristic

reading, the essence of the liberal arts hobbies, is much more difficult to find. The developing reader must discover which bookshops
(commonly small, specialized, and possibly antiquarian), public and
university libraries, and online services are apt to contain good
material.

Information about reading materials may be gained by, among
other means, taking adult education courses, consulting with librari-
ans, and – where possible – joining a special interest club. Since mass
media advertising about such materials is rare, these hobbyists are
inclined to ignore it as a source of information about new material (e.g., the blizzard of online ads from Amazon.com about new
books). Instead, they search in, for instance, the catalogs of publishers known to distribute their materials, certain periodicals with the
same reputation, and the aforementioned libraries and bookshops.

Career: Establishment

By the time the typical liberal arts hobbyists reach establishment,
they know their sources of reading material and routinely exploit
them. What remains to be routinized are the circumstances in which
personal reading can be carried out. To decide on these circumstances
is to be become established as a liberal arts hobbyist.

Among other considerations, this means finding a place to keep
books, newspapers, and magazines when not reading them. Does
such material fit decently on the bedside table, breakfast table,
reader's desk, coffee table in the living room, or other furniture?
Material read on a computer may pose a problem, in that the bigger
laptops may be too large for the space in these areas or the occasion of their use. What happens to the breakfast conversation when
one of the interlocutors becomes both focused on and eclipsed by a
computer screen?

Moreover, it is during establishment that these hobbyists come to
grips with the affordability of their hobby. Some hobbyist readers
dish out sizeable sums to feed their voracious appetite for material.
The reason for the popularity of the bargain paperback is obvious
here, as it is for affordable electronic and Internet material. Nevertheless, some readers love the hard cover editions, their feel, their
comparative elegance, their durability, and the like. The price of these
'treasures' may be barely affordable, but for them sentiment overrides
economics.

The circumstance of (un)affordability drives some readers to patronize the library, borrow from a friend, copy material (perhaps illegally), even to shoplift it. Others buy electronic copies, though they might prefer a 'proper' book or magazine. Still others turn to the used-book market, buying online or, more interestingly, hunting in the half-light of the musty brick-and-mortar, second-hand outlets. The latter may even become part of the 'must-sees' during a reader's touristic travels; for example, while holidaying in London why not explore some of its many second-hand bookshops or, in Paris, some of its *bouquinists* lined up along the Seine?

Another circumstance of committed reading is setting aside periods of time for it. What is more, these sessions must be enshrouded in the solitude necessary for effective concentration or, if done in the company of others, this state must be achieved by tuning them out. Solitude, actual or virtual, is a condition for serious reading, which, however, rests on the process of routinizing that condition. This is accomplished during establishment and becomes part of the reader's lifestyle. As is evident in the preceding section, readers try to tune out not only other people but also all other sentient distractions. Moreover, committed readers have rules they expect people who know those readers well to abide by, one being to conduct no conversation with them while they 'have their nose in a book'. Another is, when within range of a reader's hearing and seeing, to minimize intrusive activity. It is in finding solitude that the liberal arts enthusiasts strive to shape their lifestyle such that reading can be pursued with maximal reward.

Dictated by what one can or will pay for reading material joined with the levels of ease and convenience that this person has grown accustomed to, committed reading soon begins to assume a certain temporal pattern. On this matter we lack data, but it seems reasonable to speculate that some of these hobbyists read most consistently at bedtime, whereas others do so at lunch, on the train, Saturday or Sunday afternoon, and the like. What is read and when may also become routinized, as in reading the newspaper at breakfast and a novel in bed before falling asleep.

Solitary reading does not in itself generate a social world. Yet, for committed readers a social world is nonetheless possible. This is the gregarious side of their lifestyle, wherein they sometimes attend author readings, participate in book discussion groups (formal and informal), chat with friends and relatives about interesting books and articles, and so on. Being a regular in the social world of reading also means dealing with sellers of reading material and possibly with book and magazine subscription services, a rather perfunctory task when done online or even at a newspaper and magazine kiosk or in a big box, brick-and-mortar outlet. It can be much more personal, however, when done in a small independent bookshop, where personnel are often eager to discuss their goods with customers. These smaller establishments along with libraries may also become rallying points for some regulars, hangouts where they recognize each other as committed participants in this serious pursuit and with whom they sometimes discuss mutual interests. It is also common for public libraries to run book discussion groups and courses on reading, some of them specialized by genre (Styles, 2007). And as mentioned earlier, committed readers may, during establishment, expand their social world by way of some cultural tourism, documentary videos, television programs, and similar resources.

Conclusions

Hobbyists are amateurs without professional counterparts. Still, this is a rather elastic definition, for all amateur activities were started by hobbyists and some present-day hobbyist activities may become marginally professional while some others will make the full transition to being a pro-am endeavor.[14] It is important to note that, in terms of career, these two types of serious leisure amount to the two sides of one coin. Stalp (2007, p. 75, n1) illustrates this well when she observes that, in the United States, there are some professional quilters who make a living at their craft, while there are many 'master quilters' also endowed with highly advanced skills who are amateurs. On the other hand, I have treated of quilters in this chapter as hobbyists, because the scarcely researched professional wing of the activity remains scientifically obscure. Is quilting a profession in waiting, already a reasonably vibrant profession (even if we lack data on it), or is it, like barbershop singing (Stebbins, 1996, pp. 22, 47), essentially a hobbyist pursuit with but a handful of active pros?

This raises the question of how far an amateur or hobbyist can go in a fulfillment career. The answer depends on many factors, among them, native talent, drive to succeed, available opportunities to learn and improve, *and* whether participants who want to make some sort of living pursuing their passion have this option. Leisure abandonment, as observed in the preceding chapter, is possible at any point in the serious pursuits.

Abandonment, sometimes manifested as burnout, is also a distinct possibility in volunteering. Nevertheless, fulfilling careers in this field, based as they are on altruistic service to others, offer a dramatically different leisure experience.

5
Fulfilling Careers in Volunteering

The reigning definition of volunteering in the field of nonprofit and volunteer studies – it is an economic definition – states that volunteering is intentionally productive, unpaid work. Although this conceptualization is descriptively correct, it fails to recognize the variety of important forces operating in the nonwork and leisure domains of life (Stebbins, 2013a). One of those forces is the possibility of finding a fulfilling pursuit in what was defined earlier as career volunteering. The economic definition says nothing about this possibility. Instead, it raises the question of why would anyone want to work for no pay? One answer – a motivational one – is that a powerfully attractive fulfillment career is possible in substantial volunteering.

This chapter covers the six types of volunteers introduced in Chapter 1. It explores the nature of fulfillment careers in each, including the avenues by which casual and project-based volunteers may enter career volunteering. People whose career volunteering lays the foundation for movement into paid employment find devotee work there. This includes marginal volunteering, which is the subject of the Conclusion. Most such work is carried out in organizations of various sizes and will be examined in Chapter 7.

Careers in career volunteering

The volunteers considered here are 'career volunteers', with casual and project-based volunteers being considered only to the extent that the latter's activities sometimes put them on the road to serious leisure volunteering. The proposition that some volunteers find careers in their serious pursuits is not well documented, even though it was first set out over 30 years ago (Stebbins, 1982). The qualifier of 'career' is necessary to distinguish serious leisure volunteering from the volunteering undertaken as casual and project-based leisure.

The data supporting career volunteering though neither as voluminous nor as widespread as those supporting the amateur and hobbyist activities nevertheless amount to a significant contribution. This research has been conducted mostly in France, Australia, Canada, and the United Kingdom (see www.seriousleisure.net/Bibliography/Volunteering). In general, most of the research on volunteering as leisure has focused on the contribution such activity makes to volunteer organizations or to the wider community, if not both.

Committees and boards

Two, sometimes interrelated, volunteer activities occasionally complicate the symmetry of the career found in career volunteering. They are committee work and the work of boards of directors. Some committee work consists of casual volunteering, or nonwork obligation depending on point of view, as in a group of musicians who set the stage for a concert to be given by their community orchestra or the set of volunteers who agree to serve refreshments at the annual general meeting of their nonprofit organization.

Other committees, however, are the scene of serious volunteer activity. Here knowledge, experience and, possibly, skill are required for effective participation in them. A nonprofit's finance committee is a common example (where its treasurer cannot also take on this function). A committee established to plan for its future is another. Often, it appears, members of these little groups gain most of their relevant knowledge and experience on the job; their taste and talent for the committee's terms of reference being sufficient for recruitment to it. This is career volunteering in that it is serious leisure, even though normally membership in such groups lasts only a few years. Therefore, the sense of a career as experienced in growing fulfillment is truncated, especially if the term of membership is this short. In sum, we might qualify such activity as marginal career volunteering, notwithstanding that it is volunteering of considerable importance for the organization.

For volunteers serving in nonprofit organizations, the possibility exists of achieving some even loftier volunteer roles, namely, those constituting the group's board of directors (trustees). This is a special kind of career volunteering found in all nonprofit groups that organize amateur, hobbyist, or volunteer activities. The chair of the board lies at the top of this short though elite hierarchy, while being elected treasurer or secretary is also an honor (and a major responsibility). The rest of the board also basks in the prestige of having been elected to it, which puts them in a position to see their nonprofit from an unusual top-down angle.

Note that nonprofit organizations in the arts and hobbies draw on volunteers from among their members to staff their boards of directors. Thus, the board of a model railroad club is composed of elected hobbyist members, while that of a community theater is formed from its elected amateur actors. Often, this stint of career volunteering is short, since normally directors and officers of these groups are legally allowed to serve in this capacity for one or two terms only. Rare is the amateur or hobbyist activity that also offers a long volunteer career, as pursued through an evolved bureaucratic structure, often one operating on a national or international level. A main example of this formation is evident in the international community of male and female barbershop singer (Stebbins, 1996a). With this exception, and possibly a handful of others, these career volunteers on boards of directors simultaneously pursue their amateur or hobbyist passion, returning to it with unadulterated attention once no longer being eligible to serve on 'the executive' (or for personal reasons leave before this). When the serious volunteer career is shortened in this fashion, we have another instance of the marginal variety just mentioned.

Where a career is evident in 'pure' career volunteering as realized through board membership is among that small number of citizens in the community who pursue over the years successive memberships on different boards. Research data on these dedicated enthusiasts is scarce. My own experience as one of them and my informal observations of like-minded volunteers in the city of Calgary suggest that they do exist and that their contributions to the community are noteworthy. In my case, I participated at different times in four boards serving the city's francophones, two of which directed immigrant welcoming organizations and two of which directed general French-community groups. Are there not also in the large cities in the West career volunteers of this bent – community leaders – who, depending on taste, talent, and experience, serve on the boards of, among others, a string of arts, sports, or community service organizations?

Philanthropic volunteering

Philanthropic donating is evident across all six of the types of volunteering covered below. It may occur as a leisure project, exemplified in a one-off gift of money or investments in support of, for example, a building, educational program, or piece of equipment. Philanthropy becomes serious leisure when it is serial, when a person or family makes in uncoerced fashion a number of gifts over time to the same type of cause or a set of different causes.[1]

In serious leisure philanthropy, there is significant effort and perseverance, evident in for example researching the would-be beneficiary, establishing the legal basis of the gift, and arranging for the gift to be received (e.g., ceremony, publicity). The donor's social world includes the beneficiary, the relevant branch of the legal profession, supportive sources of money (e.g., banks, investment firms), and clients of the beneficiary (e.g., students, patrons, fans). The identity flowing from such largesse is manifested in some sort of public recognition of the donor (e.g., plaque, name on a building, written acknowledgement in a document).

Stages in career volunteering

Table 1.1 arrays volunteers along the vertical axis according to interest, interest in people, ideas, and human-made things and concerns of a floral, faunal, and environmental nature. This interest, as noted in Chapter 2, roots in two major conditions that comprise the love for a given core activity, namely, taste (predilection) and talent (ability). In volunteering an inclination toward working with certain kinds of people, animals or plants, for example, may seem an obvious precondition for this kind of serious pursuit. But the opposite is less so. People who, in general, want to volunteer also have particular distastes that shrink their field of acceptable free-time interests. For instance, some people detest dogs or cats, the idea of tending to plants, or the thought of helping other people. Indeed, rare is the person who can identify strongly with all six types of interest.

In any case, there is in volunteering a strong sense of altruism toward the target of benefits that motivates initial participation, with self-interest becoming the more dominant attitude later in the volunteer's career (see Gage III & Thapa, 2012). Nonetheless, Holmes (2001, p. 108) showed in her study of museum volunteers that personal interests motivate them even at the start of their fulfillment careers. Thus, they may have an interest in the museum itself or one of its collections or they may want to 'give something back to the institution'. Green and Chalip (2004) found in their study of volunteers at the Sydney Olympic Games such self-interested motives as wanting to help the event or the community, have a learning experience, and be part of the excitement.

And it was observed in Chapter 2 that taste and talent seem most of the time to go together. Yet, this combination is not inevitable, perhaps especially in volunteering, for sometimes volunteer involvements may sooner or later bring out a weakness in talent that an initial strong taste belies. How many volunteers have discovered that their interest in working with immigrants is shaken by their inability to understand the religious practices or political beliefs of their clients? How many would like, in spirit, to work building and maintaining hiking trails, only to learn once on the job that they have back problems that severely limit such a contribution?

Popular volunteer

Examples of career, or serious leisure, volunteering for other people include ski patrol, search and rescue, emergency medical worker, trained/experienced hospital volunteer, and tutor of second-language learners. The worldwide volunteer organization The Guardian Angels, which protects against crime and violence in neighborhoods, schools, and, now, cyberspace, further exemplifies this type. Mentoring is a form of serious leisure volunteering (Stebbins, 2006). Casual volunteering by serving other people is seen in, for example, ushering, handing out leaflets, collecting donations (including fundraising), giving directions, and participating in community-wide welcoming clubs (as rank-and-file member). Popular volunteering in leisure projects is evident in the various people-oriented roles volunteers fill at conferences, arts festivals, children's events, and sports tournaments.

Beginning

At the beginning stage, few if any of the popular career volunteering activities can be entered by first dabbling in them. Working with people commonly requires a priori a significant amount of training, as nearly all the volunteer functions listed above suggest. Only mentoring in that list, when conducted informally, is ordinarily done without formal instruction on how to do it. On the other hand, formal organizations like Connecting Generations in the United States offer considerable training for their volunteers (http://www.creativementoring.org, retrieved October 19, 2013). The ease with which we can engage in casual popular volunteering stands out against the requirement of training for its serious leisure counterpart.

Training for a career in a popular volunteer activity is crucial. Its effectiveness hinges on, among other criteria, how thorough it is, how inspiring it is for the beginner, and how accessible it is for that person (e.g., online versus a classroom in the center of town). Such instruction, possibly along with some practical work, is a solid psychological investment in the neophyte's fulfillment career: good training helps ensure a good leisure career.

Development and establishment

Career development here consists in substantial measure of gaining experience in the activity, part of which is learning how to put training into practice with maximum effectiveness. At this early point of the research in this area, it is difficult to generalize about the nature of its experience, for it varies immensely from search and rescue to hospital volunteering to tutoring second-language learners. Moreover, each of these areas of volunteering has numerous specialties, as in mountain, ground, and air–sea search and rescue and in hospital patient–care liaisons and orderlies serving as volunteers there. What can be said in this respect is that the core activities are complex, and that participants improve at doing them as they gain skill (where required), knowledge, and experience along the way. Their sense of fulfillment grows in parallel.

Thus advancing in popular career volunteering is mostly, if not entirely, along these lines of personal development. That is, in most areas if a formal structure of ranks exists it is relatively flat. For example, a Guardian Angel might aspire to the position of patrol leader, a search-and-rescue team member to becoming manger of the team. Informally, however, seasoned volunteers will be recognized by peers and managers for their accumulated skill, knowledge, and experience and, of course, for their willingness to serve. Clients too, the patients, students, rescued people, and the like, may also express appreciation for a job well done. In fact, for many participants, this is one of the most coveted benefits of volunteer work.

Emergency medical service offers arguably the richest set of opportunities for advancement, ultimately leading out of popular volunteering into paid employment. Although there is considerable variation around the world on where volunteering ends and the possibility of remuneration as a livelihood begins, the early positions (e.g., ambulance drivers) are commonly enacted as serious leisure. Some emergency medical technicians may serve gratis. Later positions of paramedic and those at the managerial level are filled at several ranks and remunerated.

Becoming established in emergency medical service requires finding a position in this list of functions that both generates noticeable fulfillment and stirs little desire for further advancement. This same sense of having arrived is also an indicator of reaching establishment in the other popular career volunteer activities, which, however, have either a flat or a nonexistent structure. In conclusion, careers in popular volunteering are felt in getting ever better (knowledgeable, skilled, experienced) at what one is doing there and, only rarely, climbing through a set of ranks. Meanwhile, another equally valued prize is the sense of fulfillment gained from expressing these acquisitions, one of the fruits of those careers.

Otherwise, establishment is based on the volunteer's collective image as someone who is devoted to the cause and a reliable participant in its events. This reputation, when it emerges, blossoms during development. But since such growth takes time, being so regarded in the volunteer's social world occurs as a central part of being established in it. Now, in the typical case, the volunteer is in demand, perhaps so much so that this person becomes overcommitted and risks becoming burned out. More will be said about this contingency in the Conclusion. Meantime, note that this disagreeable feature of establishment threatens all six types of volunteer.

Idea-based volunteer

Volunteering motivated by an idea or set of ideas (principle or set of principles) often gets expressed in a service of some sort. Examples in the serious pursuits are legion: pro bono legal service, volunteer consulting, volunteer retired business people advising on business, and political party volunteers working on strategy or policy. Not conceivable as a service, however, is advocacy volunteering (including protest activity), which nonetheless requires manipulating ideas, in this instance, to persuade a target group to think in a particular way. Moreover, for those wanting only a limited volunteer experience, any of these could also be carried out as leisure projects. Finally, I can think of no instances of casual volunteering undertaken by working directly with ideas, and perhaps for good reason. Casual leisure is fundamentally hedonic and, as such, is not idea-based volunteer activity as just defined.

Beginning

Since idea-based volunteering cannot be of the casual variety, it follows that, as with popular volunteering, none of these activities can be entered by dabbling in it. Elsewhere, in project-based leisure, participation may nonetheless nurture a possible fulfillment career. For instance, one might lend a hand in placing lawn signs for a candidate's electoral campaign, then become interested in a deeper and more long-term engagement, say, helping shape that person's political policy. Or a sign-carrying activist taking part in a demonstration might subsequently want to join the cause's insider core to assist with planning its future confrontational events.

Committee work, as described above, offers another possible point of entry to idea-based career volunteering. Such participation can often enhance a member's understanding of the group's mission and its implementation. Moreover, such participation may be sufficient to pull that person further into its operations, into career volunteering.

Career development and establishment

Formal training, which is part of beginning a career in popular volunteering, seems on the whole much less prevalent in idea-based volunteering. In the latter, 'training' is largely informal, more a matter of gradual personal development during which participation in the cause continues. Thus all serious participants are expected to learn as soon as possible the central tenets of the party, religion, activist cause, and so on. This is commonly accomplished by reading certain texts and tracts, watching special videos, talking with core members of the group, all being avenues of informal adult education. Formal courses and other training sessions are comparatively rare in this volunteer interest.

Obviously, none of this applies to those who volunteer their legal, consulting, and business services. These people are already highly trained and commonly well experienced. Such activity is most evident in the establishment and maintenance stages of the volunteer fulfillment career.

Bureaucratic career routes are common in idea-based volunteering. Political parties, religious organizations, advocacy groups, and other idea-based nonprofits, have administrative structures, a number of interrelated positions through which an eager volunteer might climb. Moreover, as will be elaborated on in Chapter 7, some of these are remunerated thus offering to interested volunteers a path to devotee work. The top-salaried post in a nonprofit group is the executive director who, however, is hired by its supreme authority, the board of directors and its career volunteers.

Material volunteer

It is possible that volunteer work with human-made things is the arena for the largest amount of project-based volunteering. Some material volunteers offer their skills to Habitat for Humanity as a project, as do those who donate their expertise to fix a plumbing or electrical problem at their church, prepare food for the needy on Thanksgiving Day, or help construct the set for a high school play. Examples of material volunteering as serious leisure include: regular volunteers who repair and restore furniture and clothing donated to the Salvation Army, prepare meals for the indigent, and do the book keeping for a nonprofit group. Volunteers providing water filters and electrical lighting to Third World countries are engaging in career material volunteering, as are volunteer fire fighters (when not rescuing people). Casual material volunteering refers to such activities as regularly preparing envelops for a charity's mailing campaign, picking up trash along beaches and roadsides (could also be classified as environmental volunteering), and keeping the score at adolescent sports events.

Beginning

The serious leisure activities listed above lend themselves poorly to entry by dabbling. Rather the typical participant arrives there with the skills and knowledge needed to undertake them. Not infrequently, these participants are masters of another serious pursuit such as cooking, sewing, furniture making, or do-it-yourself. Now they would like to volunteer their expertise and experience for a cause with which they identify.

An early career contingency here is learning about that cause. Since this is not an area rich in research, we can only speculate about how would-be material volunteers find their outlets. Word of mouth is one obvious way, as when a friend, relative, or colleague suggests an altruistic expression for their hobbyist talents. Others, already keen to contribute to community life through their serious pursuit, contact a cause by telephone or the Internet (Web sites often list volunteer opportunities). A third way is through recruitment. For example, a material volunteer is asked, given that person's relevant expertise, to work on the set for the high school play or fix a plumbing problem at the local mosque. Moreover, the recruited expert may be a worker rather than an amateur or hobbyist, exemplified in accountants who donate gratis their time to do a nonprofit's bookkeeping or the helpful plumber who also makes a living in this capacity.

Most serious material volunteers have already been 'trained' in their hobby, arriving at their volunteer activity ready for action. Yet, this is not true for volunteer fire fighters who must be certified through a training program (not unlike training for search and rescue). And some accountants may want to take a course on the ins and outs of bookkeeping for incorporated nonprofit organizations.

Development and establishment

Career development in material volunteering is largely a matter of gaining ever more experience in the activity and a reputation for executing it well. That experience and reputation are unique to the material volunteer activity being pursued as specialized as it is. As time goes by, fulfillment careers toward the end of the establishment stage in these pursuits consist mainly of experiencing the many personal and social rewards of such involvement. This is a period during which the participant is deeply immersed in the surrounding social world, including occasional if not frequent expressions of appreciation from the targets (the tourists) of that person's volunteer efforts.

Floral volunteer

Career volunteering in this type occurs, for example, as gardening (flowers, shrubs) for a church, community green space, friend, or neighbor. Such volunteering may be conducted indoors, where a volunteer is called upon to tend to plants in a hospital, religious establishment, community center, or senior center. Vegetable gardening for the needy also falls into this category, as does planting each season trees and shrubs to beautify a green space or the property of a community organization. As with idea-based volunteering any of these might also be pursued as leisure projects. The casual floral volunteer performs for church, community, charitable organization, and the like such altruistic activities as raking leaves, mowing lawns, watering lawns and plants, and weeding gardens.

As an example, Vancouver has a volunteer gardener program calling for all three types of floral volunteer to work in the city's diverse green spaces (retrieved November 23, 2013, http://vancouver . ca/home-property-development/gardening-on-traffic-calming-spaces .aspx). At the Ridge House Museum in Ridgetown, Ontario, Canada, volunteers are recruited to assist museum staff with planting and maintaining the flower and vegetable gardens surrounding its property. Botanical gardens everywhere have a voracious need for floral volunteers. To constitute leisure volunteering, the three types must always be seen by the volunteer as agreeable, not as unpleasant obligations.

Beginning, development, and establishment

As with their material cousins career floral volunteers arrive at their altruistic activities with requisite skill, knowledge, and experience. To be sure, they will learn even more 'on the job', but just the same they cannot dabble at it. That is, whoever engages these volunteers expects them to fill their specialized role consisting of how to plant; protect against insects; provide adequate moisture; prepare shrubs, trees, and perennials for winter; to mention a few requirements.[2] In some places, the rudiments of this knowledge base may be acquired formally, as in the three-month Master Volunteer Gardener Program offered by the Extension Division of Michigan State University (retrieved November 23, 2013, http://msue.anr.msu .edu/program/info/master_gardener_volunteer_program).

Career floral volunteers typically have no organizational structure within which to advance. That is, their development is their ever-growing stock of skill, knowledge, and experience, motivated by the fulfillment gained and anticipated from successful horticultural activity. Note, however, that some of these volunteers may also be pursuing hobbyist gardening, and some of them may want to expand this interest by volunteering in a garden club or larger organization. There they might aspire to the role of president or treasurer or that of member, if not chair, of the steering committee that runs the annual garden competition.

For these organizationally inclined volunteers and hobbyist-volunteers, establishment means achieving their desired level of community recognition for their excellence in gardening.

But there is a personal side, as well. For all gardeners, establishment refers to having gained the skills, knowledge, and experience needed to engage in fulfilling gardening throughout a typical growing season.

Faunal volunteer

Faunal volunteers work with animals, which for our purposes includes birds, fish, rodents, and reptiles.[3] Career volunteers in this type serve, among other places, at the Society for Prevention of Cruelty to Animals (Humane Society), in animal rescue units, at the local zoo, in animal rehabilitation services, and in dog-training programs. Knowledgeable people who care for someone's pet (outside the volunteer's family) on a regular basis (serious leisure) or as a one-off service (project-based leisure) are part of this type. Whereas volunteering only to feed a holidaying friend's bird or cat or walk that person's dog, assuming the experience is enjoyable, are instances of faunal volunteering as casual leisure. Chevalier, Lemancq, and Simonet (2011, p. 150) briefly discuss the role of volunteers in equestrianism, some of whom move on to become amateur or professional equestrians. Still, this is an uncommon career route for volunteers in general.

Beginning

Dabbling may someday be shown to be a most, perhaps even the most, common route to faunal volunteering. How many children or adolescents become interested in family or neighborhood pets, fauna they have seen while on a familial or educational outing or in a specimen they have observed at the zoo? This is casual observation, entertainment of sorts. But it could lead to a desire to own an animal, bird, or fish as a pet and to learning enough about maintaining its life to become a knowledgeable hobbyist (maker and tinkerer). With a love for the care and feeding of this kind of fauna and possibly the entire species, it is a plausible next step to become a faunal volunteer at one of the establishments mentioned in the preceding paragraph.

All this – the hobby and the volunteer work – requires some training. A casual leisure approach to owning a dog, cat, or pet snake is simply not enough to ensure the animal's long-term welfare. The needed knowledge may come informally from friends or relatives or from self-directed learning (e.g., Amazon.com and local public libraries are loaded with manuals on how to raise all sorts of creatures) or formally from adult education courses. Joining a group to engage in faunal volunteering will lead the participant into further training specific to its mission. This latter involvement seems not to be pursued by neophytes, however, for at that stage they usually want to concentrate on learning about their favorite fauna (commonly a pet).

Development and establishment

Somewhere in the course of acquiring knowledge, the enthusiast passes from beginning into development – the line separating the two stages being imprecise at present levels of research. Still it seems reasonable to argue that it is mostly in later development that some faunal hobbyists get interested in faunal volunteering. For them they continue to develop by acquiring the new knowledge needed for effective volunteering. Also in later development both hobbyists and volunteers often continue to advance in their technical sophistication as realized through experience.

Establishment for the career faunal volunteer consists mainly of providing a scheduled knowledge-based service for one or more of the organizations or programs like those set out above. Although participants continue at this stage to learn and profit from experience (such learning never ceases), life as this kind of volunteer is now routinized, typically becoming a central feature of their leisure lifestyle. It is possible, too, that establishment may be momentarily unsettled when the volunteer takes on a second faunal volunteer activity or abandons one to sign up for another. And, unlike popular and idea-based career volunteering, there is in the faunal type little or no hierarchy of volunteer positions to advance through.

Environmental volunteer

Environmental volunteering entails either monitoring or changing a particular set of external conditions affecting the people, flora, or fauna living in them. The change striven for is not always defined as favorable by everyone it may affect (e.g., mountain hikers might oppose a campaign by dirt-bikers for new trails in an area where the former have been enjoying exclusive use). Career volunteering here includes maintaining trout streams and hiking and cross-country ski trails as well as creating, organizing, and conducting environmentally related publicity campaigns (e.g., antismoking, clean air, clean water, antilogging or mining, and access to natural recreational resources such as lakes, forests, and ocean frontage). Any of these could also be pursued as leisure projects. The casual volunteer also finds opportunities in these examples, seen in door-to-door distribution of leaflets promoting a clean air campaign and picking up litter in a park or along a highway.

Beginning

It appears improbable that someone could enter career environmental volunteering by dabbling in it. They might do this, however, following upon casual involvement with a cause or one of its projects. By distributing leaflets, gathering litter, or just simply enjoying a natural feature, an enthusiastic participant might want to become more deeply and directly involved in protecting and preserving the environment of interest. Unless specifically invited by someone, or inspired by a mass appeal, to join an environmental project or organization, the beginner's first step is normally to contact a group whose mission gives expression to this new found passion. Once signed on as a volunteer, the newcomer and neophyte will receive training appropriate to the activity to be engaged in.

Development and establishment

Career progress during these two stages is much the same as that described earlier for faunal and material volunteering. For the most part, it involves gaining further knowledge and experience. And here, too, little or no hierarchy of volunteer posts exists that might appeal to organizationally minded people.

Mixed types

Many career volunteer activities bridge two or more of the aforementioned types. One is pro bono legal service, wherein a lawyer works with both ideas and people. Volunteer consultants have the same dual focus, as do guides and volunteer teachers and instructors in zoos and museums. Missionary work invariably centers on both ideas and people, but may also involve things (e.g., building a school, setting up a hospital). Furthermore, missionary work could extend across four types such as when its goals include working with local people to establish a source of safe water, which requires cleaning up the surrounding environment. Careers in the mixed types may be or more or less complex vis-à-vis those in the individual types of which they are composed. But the mixed types do have the advantage for those volunteers in search of it of offering an exceptionally fulfilling leisure experience.

Burnout

Burnout has been defined as physical and emotional exhaustion stemming from long-term stress, frustration, and excessive obligation in a volunteer activity (Smith, Stebbins, & Dover, 2006, p. 30). I give greatest attention in this chapter to this condition, because it is commonly associated with overexuberant volunteering (Musick & Wilson, 2008, p. 448). In fact, burnout is not confined to volunteers, but may occur in work or other leisure (serious or project-based). When burnout strikes complex leisure, the second undergoes a metamorphosis, turning into overbearing obligation and taking on a work-like quality too unpleasant to bear in an activity once embraced for its significant level of fulfillment. Burnout has much the same effect in the devotee occupations, and is disliked for many of the same reasons. By contrast, when it occurs in nondevotee work, it is largely a matter of exhaustion: putting too many hours in on the job or working at it too intensely, with too few hours available for recovery from accumulated fatigue (see 'overworking' in Kalleberg, 2007, chapter 6).

Conclusion: Marginal volunteering

Marginal volunteers feel a certain moral coercion to perform a particular volunteer activity, a sentiment unknown to the 'pure' or 'mainstream' volunteer. The first have a range of activities to choose from, but choice is substantially guided by extrinsic interests or pressures (Stebbins, 2001b). So what are their motives? Are they volunteering for the rewards that come with pure volunteering or are they motivated by those rewards and some others? Put this way: would they volunteer for the group were there no reimbursement of expenses? Would they volunteer for that group were there no in-kind payments of the sort they have been receiving or have been promised? Some would-be volunteers might have to answer the first question negatively, because the expenses are too great to bear. They would have to forego the rewards of this kind of leisure (and possibly certain other kinds, too), because they lack the money needed to participate.

But what about the second question? The attraction of in-kind payment, and let us now add, monetary payment, push to center stage another sort of reward for volunteering, for this form of leisure. To the extent that the volitional definition is valid (presented in Chapter 1), that people volunteer as a leisure activity, we would not expect them to be interested in making money from it. Indeed, it is normally the opposite: we are accustomed to spending money to engage in leisure, and where we do not do this, as in pursuing nonconsumptive free-time activity (e.g., sunning on a beach, going for a walk, taking a nap), making money from it is not on our minds. It seems, then, that a desire to turn a volunteer activity into one that, in some way, is or will be lucrative or otherwise extrinsically beneficial finds participants redefining the activity as one that should also relate directly to their livelihood. It is thus that we may speak of marginal volunteers, who by the way make up only a 'small minority' of all volunteers (Musick & Wilson, 2008, pp. 61–62).[4]

Nonetheless, marginal volunteering as just described can be a stage (beginning or developmental) in a fulfillment career. Students who perform unpaid or poorly paid intern work as one of the requirements for their professional degree constitute an example. Another is when people volunteer in hope that their experience in the activity will enhance their qualifications for a related remunerated post (e.g., Holmes, 2006). This 'volunteering' is at bottom obligated activity, albeit some participants may also find it intrinsically rewarding and therefore quite attractive. For them it is essentially a serious pursuit. Whether nonwork obligation or leisure we must regard such marginal volunteering as a possible (not always leisure) step in a fulfillment career.

6
Professional Devotee Work

Professional work has great allure. Some of it is alluring because it is widely seen as prestigious, well paying, and intensely interesting. Here is the best of all occupational worlds. Other such work, however, is just as alluring, even though some of it is less prestigious, pays less well, but is nonetheless also intensely interesting. Law and medicine are archetypical examples of the first. Famous painters, musicians, and writers exemplify the second; they have high prestige, intensely interesting work, but in most cases poorer remuneration. Nevertheless, many in this second group, though they have intensely interesting work, are comparatively weakly paid and have more ordinary public regard. Thus, for every celebrated painter or writer, there are hundreds of more ordinary counterparts. The latter make a modest living at their art, keep body and soul together by supplementary employment, or are helped by the greater earnings of an employed spouse or partner (see also Gutting, 2013). They are part-time professionals (see later). And there are at least as many amateurs, some of whom are of professional quality.

This chapter explores the late-establishment, maintenance, and decline stages of the fulfillment career as they are experienced by amateurs and client-centered and public-centered professionals (defined in Chapter 1). Before considering the three stages we must, however, look at the main concepts that will organize our discussion.

Professionals and amateurs

As said already, all these professionals started as amateurs, but at a point in later establishment turned professional or begin thinking about doing so. This is a critical point in the fulfillment career, but only for some amateurs. That is, most never consider, or reject the possibility of, making a living at their pursuit. Others give the matter some thought, flirt with the idea (e.g., temporarily quite their day job), but eventually drop it. A small proportion push ahead, however, though frequently doing so with notable struggle and ups and downs.

Since it is unnecessary for the purposes of this book to wade into the controversy that has emerged around the sociological definition of professional (for a review, see Harper, 2007, pp. 223–224), discussion will be guided instead by a dictionary definition of profession. The *Shorter Oxford English Dictionary* (2002 edition) defines it as 'a vocation, a calling, *esp.* one requiring advanced knowledge or training in some branch of learning or science...*gen.* any occupation as a means of earning a living'. According to this definition, the professions are but one class of occupation. Other dictionary definitions add, in harmony with the first part of the OED definition, that because of their high reputation, the professions nevertheless constitute a very special class.

Still, the matter is rather more complex than the dictionary definitions allow. Does a calling, or vocation, refer to serving a clientele – the client-centered professional – or to serving a public – the public-centered professional? Amateurs in art, science, sport, and entertainment who seek to make their passion a livelihood are hoping to become public-centered professionals.

As for the students in training for the client-centered professions, they may be conceptualized as 'pre-professional' amateurs (Stebbins, 1979, p. 36). They are aiming for a career in those professions, sometimes referred to as the 'liberal' professions. Theirs is a calling to serve a target clientele as done by, for instance, physicians, lawyers, accountants, engineers, and architects. These students when they succeed in their formal training are formally certified (licensed) for their achievements. Now they may legally practice what they have learned.

These pre-professional student-amateurs take courses sequenced into larger specialized formal programs, engage in practical work, and thereby learn just how fulfilling their future profession can be. In this milieu they develop a substantial devotion to their future profession. The practical work gives them the opportunity to do at least some of the core tasks done by their professional counterparts. All this occurs in an atmosphere that is essentially one of serious leisure, in that students can and do at times quit these training programs, giving substance to their basically uncoercive nature. Moreover, there is evidence that they love what they do.

> Many students say they are pursuing their subject out of love, and that education is an end in itself. Some give little thought to where the qualification might lead. In one study of British PhD graduates, about a third admitted that they were doing their doctorate partly to go on being a student, or put off job hunting. Nearly half of engineering students admitted to this.
>
> (*The Economist,* 2010)

But are there not students in these programs who feel obligated to be there, as by parental pressure or a desire to make money however disagreeable the training required by this goal? Probably so. For them being a student seems best described as a nonwork obligation.

The analogous situation for amateurs learning the public-centered professions is much fuzzier. Chapter 3 shows that informal and adult-education-style learning suffices for many of the four types of amateurs. Nevertheless, in art and science, participants may acquire college or university diplomas in their passion, the majority of them hoping to find work in it, to become public-centered professionals. True, the diploma is a kind of certification. But it is also true that uncertified amateurs are also pursuing – sometimes quite successfully – the same artistic or scientific activity. In other words, the public-centered pros lack the substantial degree of control over who enters their callings that the client-centered pros enjoy (Stebbins, 1992, pp. 28–30).

Going professional

For many people whose fulfillment careers carry them into professional work, this transformation begins, sometimes abruptly, with their decision to try to make a living in the activity. Thus the line between development and getting established can be much sharper for professionals compared with most amateurs. Yet, going professional and getting established as such in the art, science, sport, and entertainment fields are at least as often imprecise periods in the fulfillment career, which is already buffeted by uncertainty and hesitation. For instance, landing an employment contract with a symphony orchestra or sports team immediately gives the new professional a substantial amount of remunerated work, though that person will also be on probation for a specified period of time.

Moreover, going professional may be further shaped by the occupation itself. Some devotee fields, among them, ultimate Frisbee (*The Economist*, 2013b) and bioethics (https://www.bioethics.ca/professionalization.html) are in the process of professionalizing. The success of this quest invariably affects (favorably, its proponents hope) the remunerative possibilities of the would-be professionals. Additionally, sources of remuneration may change for better or worse. For example, the Competitor Group, organizer of more than 80 high-profile races, has quit paying appearance fees to elite road runners (Pilon, 2013). Road running is currently barely professional, in that appearance fees are generally meager, though income from sponsors can be more substantial.

Public-centered professionals

Consider first the area of fine art. The professional careers of artists are so varied that they have so far defied description, even in general fashion. The best that can be done, given our present knowledge, is to note some of the differences between individual- and group-based careers in art. In the first category, we find such creative people as writers, painters, sculptors, and jazz singers. To get established, they must acquire a sufficiently good reputation to be considered professional according to the standards used by established professionals in their art world (Becker, 1982, chapter 1). For the later three, this reputation usually develops first on a local level; that also holds true for writers unless their works are more widely distributed. The establishment stage feeds on success at major turning points; one must, for example, place well in juried exhibitions or performances of the art; gain the favor of such critical mediators as art dealers and chain bookstore owners, who can then bring the participants' works to the public's attention; and receive invitations to contribute to selected displays of the art in question, for example, at art shows, writers' fairs, museum exhibits, and jazz festivals (Rosenblum, 1978; Gibbons, 1979; Sinha, 1979; Simpson, 1981, chapter 3; Basirico, 1986; Craig, 2006).

Overall, getting established in the individual arts means learning from experience, learning what brings acceptance and rejection from the art world and its public. Getting established also means adding to the foundation of skill and knowledge on which expression of the art rests. The artist knows the basics, having acquired them in development, but improvement beyond that base is infinitely possible as well as a measure of one's standing in the field.

All I have said here about individual artists holds for those in groups, except that getting established generally means moving within or between collectivities. Symphony musicians, for example, get established by acquiring more responsible and better paid positions within their instrumental section (e.g., moving to principal player) and by moving from less to more prestigious orchestras that also offer longer seasons and better pay (Westby, 1960; Faulkner, 1973). A similar pattern can be observed in dance (Sutherland, 1989, pp. 103–104; Sulcas, 2007). In theater, as the thespian's reputation grows, so too do the number of invitations to try out for lead roles in major productions. Individual jazz musicians may also move from less to more prestigious ensembles or the ensemble may itself grow in stature over the years (e.g., the Basie and Ellington bands). For a few group-based artists, the process of becoming established may last until they attain the status of soloist or principal and, thus, the opportunity to pursue their art on an individual level.

One common thread running through the establishment stage for many fine artists, whether individual or group-based, is the Circe of commercialism. In part, it may be necessary to 'go commercial' simply to make a better living when income from purely artistic work is meager, a condition created by a combination of low public demand and acute oversupply of the art (Seltzer, 1989, p. 223). Thus, the jazz musician may have to play dance gigs, the singer may have to work in radio commercials, the actor may have to accept parts in dinner theater, the painter may have to produce water colors for corporate offices (Stebbins, 1962; Federico, 1974; Rosenblum, 1978, p. 32; Simpson, 1981, pp. 58–59; Craig, 2006, p. 87). At this stage, an unknown, but probably high, proportion of professionals succumb substantially, even entirely, to the attractions of an enhanced standard of living made possible by these outlets for their talents (in painting, see Cotter, 2014).[1] To the extent this happens, they leave behind the fine art side of their occupation as well as the public and professional respect accorded to those who shun commercialism. They may, however, make a name for themselves in entertainment (in jazz see the career of Miles Davis described in Larkin, 1999, pp. 230–231).

Another common thread is assessment as a career turning point; witness the audition in the performing arts, the jury assessment in the visual arts, and the evaluation in the literary arts. All artists, both amateur and professional, submit to these assessments during the established stage; many continue to do so well into the maintenance stage and some, particularly writers and actors, continue to the end of their careers (in acting see Levy, 1989, p. 122). In every instance, artists provide a sample of their work, whether by performing a part, showing paintings or photographs, or submitting a manuscript to an individual or committee who then judges its quality. Those who review the sample are true 'gatekeepers', in the sense that their judgments lead to acceptance – perhaps an orchestral position, a published short story, or a table at a craft fair – or rejection, with its painful message that the artist must seek success elsewhere.

Finally, the 21st century, with its abundance of electronic technology, has forced most musicians in the fine and entertainment arts to be evermore enterprising (salaried musicians are sometimes an exception). Thomson (2013) found in her study of American musicians that they must now, to have a decent living, fill a number of roles and draw income from a variety of sources. They must work as free agents using wherever they can and to their advantage the relevant electronic technology. Becoming established requires musicians to meet these career contingencies, which Thompson found the successful ones liked doing.

Discussion of the careers of professional scientists is limited here to those in 'institutional' settings: institutes, universities, and research centers. It is their work that is most likely to be published in places where amateurs can find it and subsequently contribute to the same body of knowledge. Mission-oriented scientists working in government or industry seldom have amateur counterparts (beyond the student stage). Both categories, however, have a clear-cut entry into the establishment stage via the research degree, typically a master's or doctoral degree, the 'calling card' for professional employment.

Professionals in institutional settings strive to establish their careers by cultivating reputations as worthy contributors to one or several specialties within a discipline.

Presentations of their research at major conferences and its subsequent publication in respectable journals or in books published by reputable houses are the main ways to accomplish this. Promotion to the rank of associate professor (in North America) is also a reasonably valid indicator of passage from the establishment to the maintenance stage. Such promotion usually means that the scientist has developed a research program of some value to his or her discipline, contributed to it sufficiently by means of publications, and is therefore viewed as willing and able to continue this routine for many years. It goes without saying that this is a time of nagging insecurity.

Receiving research grants and fellowships, awards for research excellence, and prestigious speaking engagements are among the ways that establishment is nurtured in institution-based science. In addition, a high rate of output of publications of acceptable quality will accelerate progress to the next career stage. Excellence in such activities as teaching (in universities) and administration are two other ways of measuring merit, although they are widely seen as less important than the ability to contribute directly to the growth of the science. Mahoney's (1976, chapters 4 and 5) review of the scientific career indicates that here, too, there are gatekeepers, such as editors, referees, deans, and department heads, who affect the practitioner's career progress.

In sport, the establishment stage begins when a player is hired by a professional team or placed on the professional list in an individual sport. This is a major turning point, although in team sport it is contingent on such chance factors as the quality of competitors for the position and the availability of positions. For similar reasons, getting drafted to a team and being invited to its training camp is, technically speaking, a pre-establishment, contingent turning point.

Whereas professional athletes must always compete for their place on the professional list or team, data from the Fifteen-Year Project (Stebbins, 1992) suggest that they typically reach a point at which this competition becomes more or less routine.[2] In team sport, for example, they work their way up to a starting position, where they can feel reasonably secure that more junior players will not outdo them. Here the sports professional passes from the establishment to the maintenance phase.

As in the other areas, awards can speed progress through the establishment stage. I found players in team sports to be especially concerned about their 'stats', the set of quantitative measures for their performance (e.g., batting averages, number of pass receptions, average points per game). Other things equal the better the stats, the better the chances of winning a starting position on the team. Finally, those players who become popular with the fans are helping to establish themselves, commonly because they are seen as augmenting ticket sales.

Professional establishment in the individual sports means reaching a consistent level of winnings from meets, matches, and tournaments, such that they sufficiently offset the costs of participation and leave enough to live on. Such a level is only possible if the player continues to improve beyond the development stage, for winnings are directly related to level of placement in each tournament. Theberge (1980), Kutner (1983, pp. 252–254), and Allison and Meyer (1988) all report that, for women's professional golf and tennis, this can be highly stressful stage of their career.

The gate keeping function, as effected in the fine arts by try-outs, is also evident in team sport. During training camp and, later, during the season, coaches and personnel managers evaluate the competence of recruits as well as regular players. In individual sport, however, gate-keepers do not exist at the establishment stage, since players advance on the basis of points earned for participating and placing in different tournaments stratified by level of prestige.

Passage into the establishment stage in entertainment is typically gradual, unless the performer is hired and paid a steady wage by an organization such as a circus or chain of comedy clubs. Like the individual fine artists, the freelancing entertainers must try to improve their act and build a reputation that makes possible a steady living from the art. This calls for, among other approaches, self-promotion with flyers and posted notices, showcasing at various nightclubs, and advertising in the appropriate mass media. Some entertainers sign with a booking agent; some hire a personal manager whose job is to help them improve and find work. In all this, each hopes to advance to increasingly better paying engagements, performed in ever more prestigious and appealing locations. It may mean quitting the road to find steady work in and around a major urban center.

To succeed, artists must seek all possible experience. If remunerative work is insufficient, they may turn to busking, a common and at times risky alternative (*The Economist*, 2013b). Friedman (1990) learned that aspiring Hollywood actors in this situation often seek work in television commercials as a stopgap. Indeed, with a hat, box, or musical instrument case open to passersby, many a juggler, magician, musician, pantomime, and stunt artist has supplemented income earned from more formal gigs. Formal gigs and busking sessions provide experience and ideas for polishing an act or turning it into consistently good entertainment. It is in connection with formal gigs that entertainers encounter their species of gatekeeper: the booking agent, nightclub manager, festival organizer, and the like.

Client-centered professionals

The student amateurs, following successful completion of their training, typically seek work as independent practitioners or as members of a small or large company. Many a newly minted dentist, lawyer, physician, accountant, and counselor, for instance, 'hangs out his or her shingle', in hope of making a living by serving clients. For these devotees becoming established means building their clientele to a point where their practice is viable. Success or failure in this quest is heavily tied to such conditions as local need for their service, affordability of their fees, knowledge and experience required to effectively serve clients, and a personality that will encourage the latter to return for more help.

Student amateurs who start out in a company, whether a small partnership comprised of a handful practitioners or a large company of like-minded professionals, face some different working conditions. Thus, they often receive a salary, albeit one commonly based on the number of clients served and the nature of the service received by the latter. Affordability, local need, knowledge and experience, and personality also count here, but the financial effects of these conditions are generated by all members of the group and shared by it, though not always equally. That is, its senior members – they would be well along in the maintenance stage of their devotee career – may get a bigger cut of the annual profit.

Among client-centered professionals the six criteria of devotee work are put to their most severe test among those employed in corporations. Generally, such organizations are substantially bureaucratized (though there is ordinarily little hierarchy), possibly to a level that seriously dilutes occupational devotion. Furthermore, innovation may be hamstrung by practices that find junior professionals doing the profession's least interesting work, leaving the most appealing activities for their senior colleagues. Then, in the interest of group profit, some juniors may be extensively overworked. The 'tyranny of the billable hour', as Harper (2013) puts it, expresses this situation in big-firm law. Clients pay by the hour for their lawyers' services, while the latter are expected to generate a number of billable hours felt by many junior practitioners to be greatly in excess of what is humanly possible.

Whether a freelance or a group-based client-centered professional, perseverance and effort leading to ever more occupational knowledge and experience continue during establishment. Gaining knowledge and experience are powerful rewards, strong enough for many of these devotees to offset the disagreeable aspects of their work such as laid out in the preceding paragraph. Here, perhaps more than in maintenance, personal and social rewards keep alive the passion for the pursuit. Remuneration at the establishment stage is often relative modest, whereas later during maintenance it is often much better.

Recreational specialization

Though it might occur during development or maintenance, establishment appears to be the most common career stage for experiencing the turning point of recreational specialization (defined in Chapter 2). David Scott (2008, p. xi) observes that specialists can be characterized as highly skilled, knowledgeable, and committed; using advanced equipment and techniques; 'having distinctive orientations with regard to social and setting characteristics; and possessing a strong sense of group identification with other members of the leisure social world'. The serious leisure and recreational specialization frameworks have, independently, provided compelling descriptions about participants who identify strongly with their pursuits and whose lives center on these activities.

Specialization seems to make this attachment that much more intense, since the enthusiast has found a richly fulfilling way to pursue the larger, general activity. Examples pursued thus include for both amateurs and professionals: back-country skiing (cross-country skiing), playing string quartets (classical music), portraiture (painting), short stories (writing), and sea kayaking (kayaking). In the client-centered professions, this is exemplified by a general practice physician deciding to work only with elderly patients, a teacher turning to special education, and a civil engineer moving into a singular focus on community sanitation. Recreational specialization is an apt term even for these professionals, for their serious pursuits are essentially leisure.

In sum, the establishment stage of the public-centered and client-centered professional career is arguably the most stressful of all. For one, practitioners at this point are especially vulnerable; newcomers with high aspirations, they are naive to a significant degree about the workings of the professional world. They are also often subject to exploitation, favoritism, and capricious or poorly informed judgments concerning their ability and potential (from critics, reviewers, coaches, directors, bosses, etc.). Often, too, financial insecurity is high during this period, linked as it is to intense competition for a limited number of opportunities. Jealousy and backbiting, although problems for professionals throughout their career, are perhaps most unsettling during this establishment stage. It is no wonder that a significant, yet still unknown, proportion of practitioners abandon altogether their push to get established, either returning to amateur status or leaving the activity altogether. Clearly, if professionals are to survive to the next career stage, they must successfully navigate two important turning points: the acquisition of sufficient ability, and the marshaling of sufficient dedication (devotion).

Maintenance

During the maintenance stage, the amateur-professional career is in full bloom, in the sense that practitioners are now able to enjoy the pursuit at its greatest level of reward. In entertainment, they are typically a headliner; in academic science, at least an associate professor; in sport, a house- hold name; and, in art, a recognized and respected professional in local, regional, or national art circles. Maintenance ends with decline, retirement, career change, or death. It is the period during which the participant experiences the maximum number of rewards and the minimum number of costs, a time when life is 'good', at least when compared with what went before. Nonetheless, life during maintenance is never an unalloyed joy. Professional and amateur careers are rarely that at any stage.

Competition, for example, is always there. The practitioner is only better prepared now to meet it. Nor do jealousy, favoritism, backbiting, and capricious judgments go away. Indeed, they may actually increase. At the lofty height of maintenance, artists, scientists, and the others have simply learned to cope with these human foibles. They do, however, know the ropes better than ever: how to avoid exploitation, prevent trouble, handle competitors, find agreeable work, and the like (e.g., Kennelly, Moyle, & Lamont, 2013). Nonetheless, when exploitation is built into the activity itself, as in professional and elite sport (e.g., Beamish, 1982; Connor, 2009), escape is only partial.

Having reached the maintenance stage in no way suggests that all mountains have now been climbed. Indeed, early maintenance may be a time for professionals to map out strategies for scaling new peaks, some of which may never be conquered. Many a classical music soloist, for instance, hopes to appear in Carnegie Hall. Only a few ever do so. Every professional athlete wants to be on a team that wins the World Series, Stanley Cup, Super Bowl, or World Cup. Many retire disappointed. The Fifteen-Year Project demonstrated that maintenance, too, has its stresses, disappointments, and disillusionments. Faulkner (1975, p. 537) notes that part of the subjective career at this stage is coming to grips with these realities and with one's realistic level of success.

In certain fields, the two major contingencies are injury and sickness. Athletes, dancers, acrobats, and others whose careers are limited by declining physical capacity can be even further hindered by injury or extended illness. Such possibilities hang like the sword of Damocles over the heads of participants. In fact, an injury may not only remove players or artists from active participation for long periods of time, but can leave them in less than complete recovery – with a permanent condition that restricts physical mobility long after the period of inactivity has ended.

Another debilitating contingency, one most commonly encountered in maintenance or late establishment, is drug and alcohol addiction. A minority of athletes and performing artists succumb. The history of jazz is legendary for this sort of thing, as the lives of Chet Baker, Charlie Parker, and Billie Holiday attest. In sport (and I am not talking about use of performance-enhancing drugs) consider the drug-shattered lives of Poli Díaz (boxer – heroin), Julio Alberto (soccer player – cocaine), and Diego Armando Maradona (soccer player – heroin). Greg Risling (2007) writes about the Hollywood scene:

If a prescription needs to be filled in Hollywood, chances are celebrities can find a doctor to do it. Doctors have a long history of feeding the drug demands of the entertainment industry from Marilyn Monroe to Winona Ryder, Elvis Presley to Courtney Love. Now, California authorities are looking at a physician who reportedly prescribed methadone to Anna Nicole Smith under a fake name. The former Playboy Playmate died Feb. 8 after collapsing at a Florida hotel. The cause is under investigation.

Because many amateurs and professionals spend more time in maintenance than in any other stage of their career, they also face a number of special structural and cultural contingencies. For instance, changes abound in taxation policies, arts funding, audience tastes, team ownership, availability of research funds, television programming, and so on. As a result some professionals may be fired, whereas others may find less work than previously. To the extent that they rely on private or public sector funding, amateur pursuits are affected as well. Career security at this stage is sometimes only relatively better than during the establishment period.

As noted, the maintenance stage can end in one of four ways: death, retirement, career change, or decline. Death is self-explanatory. Retirement refers to leaving the work force, though this may be only partial. Changing careers means entering a new line of work or leisure, a line that may or may not be related to the one just abandoned. Thus, the academic scientist might become a dean, the baseball player a coach, the symphony violinist a conservatory professor, the stand-up comic a film actor. Here, too, gender may become a contingency. For example, Hanna (1988, p. 121) reports that ballerinas are conspicuously under-represented in such nondancing second careers as choreographer-composer and director-manager. So acute is the retirement problem in dance that Canada opened in 1985 the Dancer Transition Resource Centre. Roncaglia (2010) found in her study of international ballet dancers a range of responses to retirement, running from denial and alienation to acceptance and letting go. In some fields retirement may lead to continuing as a post-professional amateur or a part-time professional (i.e., with reduced remuneration). Meanwhile, career change is a common response for participants who face decline before occupational retirement is reached.

In the client-centered professions maintenance is usually the period of greatest expression of skill, knowledge, and experience combined with the highest level of remuneration for such activity. Of course, in any profession the possibility exists at any time that a new problem may present itself for which past experience has failed to prepare the expert. These occurrences are less common in maintenance then earlier, but can nevertheless be most interesting, especially when some of the ordinary work has become humdrum (e.g., giving flu shots for physicians, closing deals on developer-built new houses for real-estate lawyers).

It is usually during maintenance that some client-centered professionals and counselors leave their work organization to become full-time independent practitioners. Systematically collected data are scarce on this phase of the careers of these occupational devotees (but see Mellor, 2006). Still informal observation suggests that many of them are attracted to freelance consultation or counseling by a desire to escape the failure of organized work to meet sufficiently the six devotee criteria (Mellor, 2006, p. 128). In this new occupational status, the worker confronts many of the challenges facing independent client-centered professionals who are just starting out. Here, too, success or failure is closely tied to such conditions as the need for their service, affordability of their fees, knowledge and experience required to effectively serve clients, and a personality that will encourage the latter to return for more help.

Assuming these challenges are met it remains for independent professionals of all kinds to establish and maintain an attractive flow of devotee work. Too much of it can be dispiriting, too little can threaten livelihood and raise the question of whether quitting organized work was a good idea. It may take months, even years, to arrive at a flow of clients that generates an agreeable amount and variety of fulfilling activity while avoiding a lengthy waiting list that will surely annoy them.

Decline

Decline is most threatening in the highly physical serious pursuits where, as one anonymous wag put it, 'the road to ruin is always in good repair'. To the extent that flexibility wanes and bones break more easily in later years, hobbies like tumbling, gymnastics, alpine skiing, and white-water canoeing tend to be renounced at that time of life. Moreover, injury can sometimes set premature decline in motion. Aging, however, is probably the number one enemy and main contingency here; its effects are felt earliest in the most strenuous of the serious pursuits, among them dance, football, hockey, boxing, basketball, and soccer. Decline comes later in fields such as orchestral music, where players in their fifties may find themselves being moved further back in the section as the years go by (Westby, 1960). With aging comes waning physical power, a slow and barely perceptible process. It quietly contradicts the myth that, whether we work in sport, dance, or some other field, we have drunk from the fountain of youth and therefore have no need to worry about physical decline, especially at so young an age as 30.

At this stage of the sports career, some players confront a second contingency: the availability of lower level, professional playing opportunities as in, for example, the minor leagues in baseball and hockey and the satellite tours in tennis and golf (Ball, 1976). Unfortunately, for some sports (e.g., Canadian football and lacrosse) there are only a few scattered senior teams in existence. Hapless aging players are simply put out to pasture – relegated to the general labor market – and replaced by younger enthusiasts with a brighter and longer athletic future.

Decline and retirement in sport are somewhat easier to accept when the alternatives are appealing, when the player has prepared for an interesting second, or nonplaying, career inside or outside the game. But what second career can match the glamor, salary, and excitement of professional sport? Level of education is a contingency here, for it is usually only in jobs requiring a university or professional degree that an ex-athlete can even begin to approach these kinds of rewards. In this regard, an outstanding reputation in a professional sport may help its retirees find, although not necessarily keep, a better than average nonplaying job (Hearle, Jr, 1975, p. 507). Nevertheless, the broad picture is one of many former professionals working in blue-collar jobs at a young age, with young families to support (in soccer, see Houlston, 1982).

According to evidence at hand, the retirement comedown is likely to be severe only in high-level professional sport (Greendorfer & Blinde, 1987; Coakley, 2001, pp. 305–306). Studies of males retiring from university football and basketball (Kleiber, et al., 1987; Adler

& Adler, 1991, p. 218) and Canadian junior hockey (Curtis & Ennis, 1988) suggest that life satisfaction can be considerable after retirement, especially if the player leaves the sport on a positive note (with an award, good playing season, team championship). Satisfaction was measured by attitudes toward life in general, postretirement employment, and marital status. An investigation of retired Polish Olympians found that they had retained high social status and a significant role in social and cultural life (Pawluk, 1984). Kadlcik and Flemr's (2008) study of elite Czech athletes also showed that many of them experienced a positive transition into retirement. And Allison and Meyer's (1988) research on female tennis professionals revealed a strong sense of relief upon retirement, coupled with a desire to resume a normal lifestyle. Stier's (2007) interviews with Swedish ex-professional tennis players revealed some confusion in their role-identity, which was however, a manageable and transitory problem.

A much more nebulous contingency at this stage is *creative decline,* a problem that chiefly afflicts artists and entertainers. This condition may be a product of occupational burnout. In stand-up comedy, this can result from too many jobs on the road during which the comic, instead of 'killing' the audience with laughter, performs on 'automatic pilot' (Stebbins, 1990). In artistic burnout expression of the art becomes routine, humdrum; it is dull for both the public and the artist. Soon the former react to the stagnation, and the latter's opportunities to produce or display his or her art diminish sharply. To reverse this trend, the practitioner must somehow find inspiration, whether by developing new material (entertainment), playing new works (music), or acting in a different genre of drama (theater).

Moreover, entertainment and even fine art can be somewhat faddish, in that certain styles may come and go with alarming rapidity. Adler (1975, p. 364) argued that, for today's painters, 'the period between the initiation of innovating or even deliberately provocative works and their final appearance and eventual eulogy by formerly conservative cultural institutions such as museums and established critics has radically contracted'. This is because vanguard artists are the elite of today's art world, which means that fashionable art becomes 'obsolete' (loses its public appeal) as soon as another innovation hits the market. This set of circumstances signals the beginning of career decline, unless the artist can rebound with still another exciting innovation. As Simpson (1981, p. 76) observed, in the art world 'originality, more than the mastery of craftsmanship, is the key to success'.

But one substantial attraction of many amateur-professional pursuits, especially those outside sport, is that practitioners can often elude decline and even forced retirement. They persist into ripe old age as full-time professionals, among them, Pablo Casals, Vladimir Horowitz, Albert Einstein, George Burns, Bob Hope, and Ernest Hemingway. Many a local amateur has followed the same path. Alternatively, the enthusiast may reduce involvement to some degree, moving to part-time professional status where it is possible to continue to make money, or to postprofessional amateur status where participation is now done purely for its fulfillment. All in all, there are a number of routes to follow should a participant move beyond the career stage of maintenance.

Conclusions

Professionals have long been known for the special orientation they hold toward their work. This orientation, which may shared by the majority of members of a given profession, reaches its broadest expression in a common outlook referred to here as the *spirit of professional work* (Stebbins, 2000). This concept denotes the distinctive set of shared values, attitudes, and expectations that form around a given type of professional work, where the work itself is seen by its practitioners, as a result of their occupational socialization, as socially important, highly challenging, intensely absorbing, and for these reasons among others, immensely appealing. This work is exceedingly complex, executed most effectively by practitioners with many years of training and experience. Additionally, the spirit of professional work pervades the work lives of a sufficient number of employed professionals to constitute an important part of their occupational subculture. Thus, from what is known through research on occupations in general, this spirit, as expressed in each profession, endows the culture of that profession with a special quality not found in any other profession or, more broadly, any other occupation.[3] Karp (1989, p. 751) concluded, after an extensive review, that 'one of the most consistent research findings in the social science literature is that professionals are relatively more satisfied with their work than nonprofessionals'.

The spirit of professional work contradicts the popular notion that occupational devotees are really workaholics. These days most people speak most of the time about workaholics as work addicts, either forgetting or overlooking the fact that occupational devotees also exist. Indeed, some of those they casually label workaholic may well be devotees in both thought and action. The history of the concept of workaholism and its relationship to devotee work is set out elsewhere (Stebbins, 2004c/2014, pp. 28–29). The drive for success does not mean that the behavior leading to it is uncontrollable, as true addictions are (Stebbins, 2010). Rather, the successful person in both leisure and work knows full well what it takes to succeed and, with a strong sense of control and personal competence, sets out to reach this goal. He or she *is* in reasonable control of an unfolding career personally designed to achieve identifiable rewards. This chapter attests this proposition. In other words, the drive for success is carried out by way of a variety of positive activities. In contrast, addiction itself, as defined in Stebbins (2010), is negative – an unpleasant state. Here, addiction-related behavior brings only temporary relief. Furthermore, this hardly sounds like an antecedent to the success and self-fulfillment to which people aspire in the various devotee occupations. More will be said about these matters in Chapter 8.

7
Hobbyist and Volunteer Devotee Work

We will follow in this chapter the same framework set out in the preceding one as it bears on remunerated hobbyist and volunteer-inspired devotee activities. As regards occupational devotion the opportunities for this kind of employment are murkier than for professionals, consultants, and counselors. Today, for example, automation and deskilling of blue-collar work have taken their toll (Braverman, 1974). The main outcome of this process has been that 'skill requirements have increased for some occupations and decreased for others, while at the same time technological change has displaced some workers from their jobs altogether' (Kalleberg, 2007, p. 50). Nonetheless, Kalleberg observes that at least in the United States the proportion of skilled craft occupations – our devotee trades-workers – has 'remained fairly constant during the twentieth century' (2007, p. 48). Meanwhile, compared with the today's trades, the contemporary world of small business appears to offer many more opportunities for a fulfillment career. And those opportunities are highly diverse.

We will return in the Conclusions to these labor market issues. Meanwhile, we look first at fulfillment careers in the skilled trades, move next to those in small business, and finally to those springing from volunteering (career, casual, and project-based).

The fulfilling trades

A trade is a devotee occupation requiring a significant level of skill and knowledge for its execution. It is commonly contrasted with semiskilled and unskilled labor and, today, usually requires formal training and certification. Framed in the SLP the vast majority of trades-workers gain entry to their devotee work through educational programs in which they may be conceptualized as student hobbyists. Still, in contrast to the preprofessional amateurs discussed in the preceding chapter, some of these students came to their training program from a pure hobbyist background.

The following trades, all practiced in modern times, are capable of generating occupational devotion:

- baker,
- barber,
- barista (coffee),
- brewer,
- bricklayer,
- butcher,
- cement mason,
- chef,
- electrician,
- gardener,
- gunsmith,
- hairstylist,
- handyman,
- jeweler,
- landscaper,
- locksmith,
- mechanic,
- metalsmith/tinsmith,
- painter/decorator,
- plumber,
- stonemason,
- tailor,
- tool and die maker,
- watchmaker (and repair),
- welder.

Although this is not an exhaustive list, it does paint a decent picture of the landscape of the modern devotee trades. Trades, or handicraft, workers produce their products and services with their hands.

Though certain kinds of knowledge are important for them, they are not essentially knowledge-based workers, in the way that the service specialists are in, for instance, medicine, computers, and electronics who now often attend the same vocational schools as trades-workers.[1] And, as in the other three types of devotee work, this type only offers the possibility of finding occupational devotion in employment that meets the six criteria. Meanwhile, many a plumber, electrician, and bricklayer, for instance, winds up in a hum drum job that pays well, is secure, but nevertheless presents too little challenge, too little fulfillment, for that person's accumulated skill, knowledge, and experience.

Getting started

Since every trade is pursued with the intention of creating a physical product and possibly a related service, its practical nature tends to obviate disinterested playful dabbling.[2] Moreover, even to execute the craft at its minimal level of expertise, requires some preliminary formation. This training need not be formal, however, but rather may be informal, of the self-directed variety (adult education). So, the first-time handyman visits a Web site to learn how to fix a leaky faucet; the first-time chef gets advice from a cookbook on how to prepare an omelet; the first-time residential landscaper reads one of the many do-it-yourself books on the subject.

Such projects might be driven by necessity, when initially defined as nonwork obligations. And they might in future lead to similar obligatory projects. Yet, it is also possible that the projects are undertaken as agreeable activities, however necessary they are. Now, to the extent that such projects are agreeable – are project-based leisure – the participant may be positively inspired to repeat the experience, possibly on a routine basis. Thus, the budding hobbyist handyman then decides to try her hand at caulking around a window frame; the chef takes up next a more complex egg dish; the landscaper embellishes his basic plan with a rock garden.

These three activities and all the others in the list above admit the possibility of participation guided by self-directed learning (through Web sites, books, magazines, informal advice, adult education courses, etc.). To this end, Amazon.com sells hobbyist books on every trade in our list. Additionally, Web sites abound, and friends and relatives may be on hand to supply informal advice (even mentoring) or ignite interest in the activity. In short, it is certainly possible to get started informally in these skilled trades, which then motivates some participants to pursue one or more of them as a livelihood.

Going to school

A skilled and experienced hobbyist in one of these trades might succeed without formal schooling in making livelihood of it much as do the independent professionals described in Chapter 6. Word could spread locally about this person's expertise, service orientation, fair business dealings, and the like such that a living becomes possible doing what was earlier purely a leisure pursuit. How common this kind of career is today has, so far as I know, never been determined. But recorded examples do exist. Tara Jamieson turned her garage-based hobby of refinishing furniture into a small business operating out of a workshop, office, and store located in another part of town (Toneguzzi, 2012). She has now quite her full-time job as an accountant. Neil Herbst met his soon-to-be business partner in a course on home-brewing. Together, they invested their savings in a microbrewery that is now a success (Mah, 2012). Herbst had been a governmental policy analyst before being let go, a consequence of budget cuts in the civil service.

The common alternative route today, as opposed to the apprenticeship system of the past, is to obtain a diploma from a trade, technical, or vocational school certifying through formal examination successful completion of a two- to five-year postsecondary program of study in a skilled trade.[3] The length of a program depends substantially on the complexity of the field. Apprenticeships, though less common, are still possible nowadays as are in-plant training programs and on-the-job training from a qualified employee. Some trades-workers gain their formal training in the military. Graduation from such programs may bring for those who intend to work for various employers and at various locations the need to join a craft union or a more broadly inclusive industrial union. Moreover, such organizations may offer their own training programs on an apprenticeship basis.

Whichever route is taken most trades-workers, with or without earlier hobbyist experience in their passion, appear to pass through a formal training program on the way to jobs where they will further polish their skills, develop their knowledge, and accumulate more experience. Nonetheless, these career paths do not exhaust all possibilities. Another is to start a business selling the products created in one or more crafts and doing so either after vocational education or instead of it (exemplified above). In the latter situation the proprietors are confident that what they make as a hobby has market value sufficient to produce a decent living, or at least a significant part of it. Thus, Frances Strathern opened her jewelry studio after completing her formal education in jewelry and metals, in this instance, at an art school (Toneguzzi, 2013).

Development and establishment

In general, there is little in these two stages, whose boundaries are indistinct, that differs from their counterparts in the professional, consulting, and counseling devotee occupations. The typical pattern is one of gaining skill, knowledge, and experience, of becoming ever more capable of delivering a quality product and related service under a wide range of conditions and demands. From the standpoint of devotee work, a main challenge facing all the devotee pursuits discussed so far is to avoid the conditions that can undermine that activity.

In addition to such personal improvement trades-workers develop and establish their occupational devotion by finding an attractive range of different opportunities in which to be innovative or creative. Carpenters, electricians, and plumbers, for example, commonly fail here when they build housing or apartment units having little variation in floor plan. Rather they can meet these devotee criteria when working on uniquely (architecturally) designed buildings. The jewelry artist just mentioned finds fulfillment in creating custom pieces for individual customers as a gunsmith does in refinishing or modifying a firearm to suit a particular client. Auto mechanics find scant fulfillment in changing oil or even sparkplugs, whereas difficult-to-solve problems (e.g., car will not start, truck has an electrical short) turn them into detectives where insight, knowledge, and experience are immense assets.

As have we seen throughout this book, in any form of devotee work fulfillment is impossible every moment of every day. So, a common goal in development and establishment in the skilled trades, as in other devotee fields, is to maximize the fulfilling activities while minimizing those that are significantly less so. The search for this balance occurs primarily during establishment, and rests substantially in the hands of the individual (personal agency). In short, it is up to the worker to find (and keep) fulfilling jobs.

Nevertheless, context also shapes this search. Thus, exciting carpentry, plumbing, and electrical work may not be available in some communities and some workers there may be in no position to move to greener occupational pastures. An interest in fulfilling gun modification and restoration might well be more difficult to realize in a pacifist culture where hunting with firearms is unpopular vis-à-vis where such hunting is common and a compatible culture of gun ownership is entrenched (e.g., the North American Rocky Mountain West). And what is the future of the skilled coffee barista in the face of the recent proliferation of push-button espresso machines?

Maintenance and decline

For the skilled trades-workers who find occupational devotion, maintenance is generally a period of steady employment at their passion. Nevertheless, economic changes can bring a shortage or a surfeit of work and thereby temporarily disturb this pattern and, possibly, the income level of the worker. Indeed, part of the challenge at this stage is having sufficient resiliency to adapt to new techniques and market demands (e.g., changing tastes, availability of materials). Being resilient is a special manifestation of the worker's innovativeness, itself a source of pride. Thus, a watchmaker might take pride in learning how to make electronic timepieces to meet a new demand from customers, even though being formally trained in making only the mechanical variety.

It is usually during maintenance that some veteran trades-workers become interested in serving their union as an official (e.g., president, secretary, treasurer). In large unions this is a salaried full- or part-time job. Full-time positions take their incumbents away from their devotee skilled trade, putting them on the road to a new administrative career. The same happens with trades-workers who establish a multi-employee company that grows to a point where the founders must spend their working hours running the enterprise. Additionally, some of these workers may become interested in teaching their trade, as in adult education classes or vocational school programs. These interests are usually part time, however; they allow continued pursuit (part time) of their craft.

Movement into one or more of these three activities could itself be considered a sign of decline, in that it might reflect abandonment of the devotee activity. Moreover, craft work is physical work, and since eyes, muscles, bones, and the like normally deteriorate with age, so will the participant's capacity to engage in that work. Indeed, such conditions may be a cardinal reason for seeking the sort of involvements described in the preceding paragraph.

Small business

A small business may be defined in many ways, including by number of employees, annual budget, and overall worth. Furthermore, what is officially considered small business varies from country to country and is sometimes referred to as informal business. Using the latter distinction research in Ukraine (Williams, Nadin, & Rodgers, 2012, p. 534) found that 'serious leisure' businesses in that country comprise about 20 percent of all informal enterprises. The definitional dimension of central concern to the SLP is number of employees and the allied question of what its upper limit is, after which occupational devotion is adversely affected.

It is presently impossible to answer this question precisely. But, as a start, let us say here that in SLP terms a small business is a kind of small group. According to Back (1981) any small group is

> small enough for all members to interact simultaneously, to talk to each other or at least to be known to each other. Another requirement is a minimum conviction of belonging to the group, a distinction between 'us', the members of the group, and 'them', the non-members. (p. 320)

Specialists in group research classify as a small group any formally or informally organized unit of two to twenty individuals. The upper numerical limit is imprecise. Nonetheless, whatever the number of members, a group becomes 'large' when regular interaction is substantially limited and intimacy is no longer experienced; the group becomes large when the amount and quality of intermember communication are diluted (Stebbins, 2002, pp. 17–18). Thus small businesses as small groups foster occupational devotion when they obviate bureaucratization and create an agreeable, productive work environment (criterion 6).

Elsewhere (Stebbins, 2004c/2014, pp. 13–17) I explore eleven types of small businesses. The aforementioned consultants, counselors, and skilled craft workers operating as small businesses, are clear examples of occupational devotion in this area. But what about other types of small businesses, where occupational devotion is also reasonably common? We can only speculate, since data are scarce. What is more, this is a difficult area in which to study occupational devotion, for there are also many small entrepreneurs who feel very much enslaved by their work. The differences separating devotees from nondevotees in small business hinge primarily on seven criteria, perhaps more: efficiency of the work team and the six criteria of occupational devotion described earlier (skill/knowledge/ experience; variety; creativity/innovativeness; control; aptitude/taste; social/physical milieu). Ten types of devotee small business (excluding consultants, counselors, and craft workers) are described below, after which we consider the distinctive nature of the devotee career in this field.

Teaching as a small business is distinct from professional teaching in primary and secondary schools and institutions of higher education. It also differs from presenting the occasional adult or continuing education course, something usually done as a sideline. Rather teaching as a small business centers on a practical interest, the demand for which is sufficient to constitute a livelihood for an instructor or small group of instructors. Thus, small businesses have been established to teach people how to ride horses, fly light aircraft, and descend to earth in a parachute. Many local dance studios fall into this category, as do driver training schools. Innovativeness here revolves around adapting lessons to the needs of individual students and their capacities to learn the material of the course.

Custom work, compared with other small business fields, provides especially fertile soil for cultivating self-fulfillment. Here, to meet the wants of individual customers, the devotee designs (in consultation with the customer) and sometimes constructs distinctive and personalized new products. Examples include workers who make their living designing and assembling on order special floral arrangements (e.g., bouquets, centerpieces) or gift baskets or confecting such as items as specialty cakes, cookies, or chocolates. Tailors, tatooists, hair stylists, makeup artists, and furniture makers, when working to the specifications of individual customers, also belong in this category. Alternatively, individual customers may be seeking a reshaping or remodeling of something they already possess, such as custom modifications to, as we just saw, a gun, watch, or item of clothing.

Animal work, though less prevalent than custom work and possibly even less so than devotee handicraft, nevertheless sometimes meets the seven criteria of devotee small business. The main examples here, of which I am aware, are the people who make a living training or showing, cats, dogs, or horses. Just how passionately this work can be pursued is seen in Baldwin and Norris's (1999) study of hobbyist dog trainers.

Evidence that *dealers in collectibles* can be occupational devotees also comes from the field of leisure studies, where the love for collecting has been well documented (e.g., Olmsted, 1991). Dealers and collectors work with such items as rare coins, books, stamps, paintings, and antiques. Still dealers are not collectors; that is, their collection, if they have one, is not for sale. But even though dealers acquire collectibles they hope to sell for extrinsic speculation and profit, they, like pure collectors, also genuinely know and appreciate their many different intrinsic qualities. Thus, when such collectors face the opportunity to sell at significant profit items integral to their collection (again, if they have one), these motives may clash, causing significant personal tension (Stebbins, 2004b). Here is an example of a work cost quite capable of diluting occupational devotion.

Repair and restoration center on bringing back an item to its original state. Things in need of repair or restoration and, in the course of doing so, capable of engendering occupational devotion include old clocks and antique furniture as well as fine glass, china, and crockery. There is also a business in restoring paintings. This work, which calls for considerable skill, knowledge, and experience, is typically done for individual customers. It offers great variety and opportunity for creativity and innovation.

The *service occupations* cover a huge area, but only a very small number seem to provide a decent chance for generating occupational devotion. One category with this potential can be labeled 'research services'. Though most research is conducted by professional devotees, nonprofessionals do dominate in some fields. Exemplifying the latter are commercial genealogists and investigators concerned with such matters as fraud, crime, and civil disputes as well as industrial disputes, marital wrangles, and missing persons.

The accident reconstruction expert also fits in this category. Day care and dating services along with the small *haute cuisine* restaurant and the small fund-raising enterprise constitute four other services that can generate occupational devotion, as the earlier examples suggest. And here is the classificatory location of such small business, nonprofessional consultants as those in fashion, landscape, advertising, and the relatively new field of personal coaching. By and large, however, the service sector is not the place to look for exciting, fulfilling work, in part because the service itself is often banal, even if important, and in part because of the ever present possibility of fractious customer relations.

The *artistic crafts* offer substantial scope for the would-be occupational devotee. Some are highly specialized, like etching and engraving glass, brass, wood, and marble. Others are more general, including ceramics work and making jewelry. Many people in the artistic crafts are hobbyists, who earn little or no money, whereas other people attempt to derive some sort of living from them. It is the second group, which consists of many part-time and a few full-time workers, who may become devotees. Variety and creativity are the principal defining criteria separating them from nondevotees in this field. It is one thing to turn a dozen identical pots and quite another to turn a dozen each of which is artistically unique. Those whose sole livelihood comes from the latter are often card-carrying members of the starving artist class; in a world dominated by philistines, it was observed earlier that sales of artistically different products are relatively infrequent.

Most *product marketing* is the province of organizationally based employees, working in large bureaucracies and constrained there by all sorts of rules and regulations and locked into excessive time demands not of their making. Meanwhile, some small businesses do survive in this field, and offer the product marketers there a devotee occupation. The archetypical example is the small advertising agency that, similar to the small customs work enterprises, designs and places publicity on a made-to-order basis for customers with budgets so restricted that they are unable to afford the services of bigger companies. Web site design and promotion services can also be conceived of as a kind of product marketing. Only two defining criteria appear to separate product marketers in small and large firms, namely control of time and size of bureaucracy. These two are nonetheless powerful enough to set off devotees from nondevotees in this area.

Most *planning work* is likewise bureaucratized in either governmental or medium-sized business firms. Indeed, city and town planners have been listed as professionals (Stebbins, 2004c/2014). But there are others facets to the occupation of planning that, on the small business level, can generate deep occupational devotion. Here, for instance, is the classificatory home of party and event planners, who if they seek sufficient variety, meet all seven defining criteria. The Achilles heel of this business is the level of efficiency of the work team, which if it fails in any major way, could result in disaster for the planner and a concomitant drop in sense of occupational devotion. Thus, it is one thing to plan well for some entertainment during a conference and quite another for the entertainers not to show up. Funeral planners suffer similar contingencies, by far the worst being a fumbled casket during the ceremony (Habenstein, 1962, p. 242).

The *family farm* is the final small business considered here. A dwindling phenomenon to be sure, it still nonetheless offers many owner-families an occupation to which they can become deeply attached. Though they may exploit either plants or animals, the operation must be manageable for the family. All criteria apply here, though some need explaining. Farmers must be innovative when it comes to dealing with untoward pests, weather conditions, governmental policies, and the like. As for variety they experience it in rotating crops over the years and in observing how each crop grows during a given season. Especially at harvest time, farmers lack control of their own hours and days. But there is normally a lengthy period between growing seasons, when farmers have more control over their lives. To the extent the farm is also run with hired hands, their level of effectiveness contributes to or detracts from the owner's occupational devotion. James Farmer (2012) examines, within the context of the local-food movement, 'small-scale farming' (a kind of family farming) as a genre of serious leisure (see also Amsden & McEntee, 2011, who discuss 'agrileisure').

Career

All these business people launch their enterprise from a serious pursuit in which they are proficient enough to dream of the possibility of making a living there. According to our career framework they are by this time in their pursuit well into the establishment stage, if not that of early maintenance. They have arrived at this point as hobbyists, graduates of formal training programs, perhaps both. Or they may have arrived here in search of a second career in a skilled trade or from disenchantment with a professional job. Now, the decision to try to make money from the activity, however tentative, adds a dramatic new dimension to its pursuit, namely, that of starting and running a business.

Even the decision by a hobbyist with no formal training to try to sell some pots, sweaters, or wood carvings is a business matter. What price should be asked, where should the goods be sold, how should they be marketed, and who are the possible customers number among the questions that arise. At this level the intention is not to find a livelihood in making sweaters and the like, but rather to possibly make some pin-money, help cover costs of equipment and supplies, even to test the waters to see if a larger business is feasible.

In other words, the participant's career in this serious pursuit becomes entangled in the career of the nascent enterprise. To the extent that the little business prospers and becomes a partial or full livelihood, the woodworker, planner, teacher, art dealer, and so on spends most if not all of maintenance creating and selling a hobbyist product or service for which there is now a decent demand. It prospers when these devotee workers maintain and apply their skill, knowledge, and experience in ways that sell.

Rick Spence (2013), a specialist on entrepreneurship, sets out seven 'key' challenges facing entrepreneurs at all stages of business development. (1) They must know their competitive advantages, as in value of their product or service and how it differs from that of competitors. (2) They must learn how to sell their product or service. (3) They may have to find some start-up capital. Some hobbyists in this situation borrow from a bank, take a second mortgage on their house, or find a friend or relative to finance them. Josh Wolf used crowd funding to launch a business making circuit boards for home arcade hobbyists, himself being one of them (Dirom, 2014). (4) Where the hobbyist must hire some help, finding and retaining good employees is a major challenge. (5) The price of the product or service is a crucial part of success in this field. (6) Spence advises 'staying focused'.

Be wary of launching prematurely new products or services, a process that could take time away from maintaining the quality of the existing ones. (7) Hobbyist-entrepreneurs, short of dying while running the business, must someday end their involvement in it. In other words, this commercial stage of the hobbyist career demands careful advance planning.

A successful career in a small hobbyist business is unique among devotee work careers, in general. In hobbyist business success requires that the core activity be mastered to the point of being able to make a living from it. It is during maintenance that success and the fulfillment it engenders are most evident. As for decline the business may live on with a new owner, even if the hobbyist-founder has lost the physical or mental capacity (or both) needed to make the product or service on which it is based. But possibly as common an outcome is that it is terminated for physical or mental reasons, or terminated because someone with the hobbyist skills, knowledge, and experience of the founder including that person's business acumen is unavailable for replacement.

From volunteering to devotee work

Most people who volunteer on a formal basis do so in one or more small, medium, or large nonprofit organizations (Pearce, 1993, pp. 15–16). The larger organizations function with some paid staff. They are remunerated part- or full-time employees who occupy positions to which some volunteers in the same or another (usually similar) organization might aspire. This orientation toward volunteering brings up again the question of marginal volunteering (it was first raised at the end of Chapter 5).

Earlier it was noted that marginal volunteering may be a stage (beginning or developmental) in a fulfillment career. For these participants it is essentially a serious pursuit, even though it may begin as a nonwork obligation. Whether nonwork obligation or leisure we must regard such marginal volunteering as a possible (not always leisure) step in a fulfillment career, including one that might lead to devotee work.

It is within this vast corps of organizational volunteers that we find those who use their altruistic role there to expressly explore for work in a particular segment of the job market. Sometimes these marginal volunteers hope to find employment by this route, gaining experience that will improve their chances of getting work in that field or a related one. Other volunteers simply want to explore the nature of work there or believe that volunteer experience will look good on their résumé. This less-than-pure volunteering is common practice these days, especially in the age bracket 15 to 24 (Statistics Canada, 2001, p. 37). Yet, even when people operate under pressure and obligation to find some sort of work and 'volunteer' their services as part of their search for such work, there are also those who manage to find an occupation worthy of their devotion.

On the other, hand pure organizational volunteers – those who serve primarily for the fulfillment derived from doing attractive core tasks – may be hired to fill a remunerative post in their organization that could generate occupational devotion. One such post is volunteer coordinator; it includes recruiting volunteers and matching them according to their capabilities and interests with the volunteer needs of the organization. And some pure organizational volunteers learn at close range about the fulfilling aspects of certain kinds of professional work carried out in their organization. Encouraged by what they have observed, they seek the formal training needed for this new career. A number of social workers, registered nurses, and recreational specialists appear to get started this way.

Volunteer maintenance and devotee work

Most career volunteers serving in one of the six types of volunteering described in Chapter 5 participate as volunteers in the maintenance stage. Barring such contingencies as compelling external demands or incapacitating physical problems that could force them to change their altruistic involvements, they continue in maintenance often following a now familiar schedule. They have acquired the skills, knowledge, and experience needed to routinely find fulfillment in their core volunteer activities. To be sure, unusual challenges may well appear from time to time. But these veterans usually have the background to meet them, doing so with enthusiasm and as an expression of their seniority in the area.

Still, career volunteering seems rarely, if ever, to lead directly to devotee work as a paid extension of the volunteer's core activities. Among the serious pursuits the path of career volunteer to devotee worker stands out from the paths running from, for instance, amateur to professional actor or football player or even hobby-ist collector to art dealer with its parallel business career. Rather, in devotee work springing from volunteering, career continuity is achieved in finding remunerated activities that are consonant with the (former) volunteer's values. Thus, through volunteering with a Scout troop, the participant lands fulfilling paid employment with the Scout Movement, say, as an instructor. This volunteer finds it deeply rewarding to be working with youth, and that post enables continued expression of this value. Nevertheless, the new employee must successfully complete a training program, since the earlier volunteer activities will have failed to prepare this person for the responsibilities ahead.

Casual and project-based leisure

These two types have generally been portrayed in this book as distinct catalysts in the fulfillment career. Dabbling is casual leisure, whereas project-based leisure is commonly a one-off encounter with an ama-teur, hobbyist, or volunteer event. Either type is capable of directly sparking an interest in greater and deeper involvement in that kind of leisure.

But, when it comes to entering devotee work by way of vol-unteering, the catalytic effect of casual and project-based leisure becomes more indirect and hence more complicated. For example, casual volunteering once a week at the local zoo familiarizes the par-ticipant with the routine of that organization and, to the extent that this person likes the zoo's routine, mission, social and phys-ical environment, and so on, he or she could become interested in long-term employment there. True, devotee jobs, as is evident in this chapter, require skill, knowledge, and eventually experience. Perhaps the participant already has a Bachelor of Arts or Science degree, a requirement for some of the zoo's employees. Alterna-tively, the goal of working at the zoo might encourage this would-be employee to go to school to obtain the needed diploma. Of course, it could also happen that this casual volunteer, enamored of the zoo's animal and human environment, is simply motivated to look for any employment there and not necessarily the kind that generates fulfillment.

Volunteering in a leisure project sponsored by an organization can lead in the same direction. Science and art museums typically mount a number of special exhibitions each year, for which volunteers are regularly sought. Likewise for sports events, the sponsoring organizations often being one of the following: a government (local, regional, national), an international body such as the international sports federations, the Olympic Movement (includes games, commissions, conferences, etc.), or a world regional games association (e.g., Pan American Games Movement, European Games, Pan Arab Games). From having volunteered in a sports event sponsored by such an organization, thoughts of being employed there could emerge, thus putting in motion a set of steps similar to those taken through casual leisure participation.

All these employment opportunities (both devotee and nondevotee) are found within nonprofit organizations. Remuneration here is normally low here compared with equivalent work in government and for-profit business. Nonetheless, both sport and culture cut a respectable figure in modern social life. Working for a sport or cultural nonprofit bestows a degree of prestige on its workers, even when their core activities are not fulfilling.

Conclusions

The devotee occupations, a significant proportion of which are found in the knowledge industries, will surely continue to be an important part of the economy of industrialized countries. Nevertheless, the scope of devotee work has shrunk in several ways. It has been buffeted by such forces as occupational deskilling, degradation, and industrial restructuring (e.g., downsizing). Deindustrialization (e.g., plant closure and relocation), failed job improvement programs, and overwork, whether required by employers or sought by workers craving extra income, have also taken their toll. Still, certain forms of devotion are more evident today than heretofore, seen for instance, in the rise of the independent consultant and counselor and the part-time professional. Nor is there any reason to suspect that small businesses or skilled trades-workers will decline in either proportion or absolute number. Yet, there are constraints on professionals of the kind considered earlier.

So, the problem appears to be less one of continued devotee work opportunities than one of a narrowed recruitment pool of people to fill those opportunities. More precisely, new jobs will be created in significant number, but only in the knowledge sector where high levels of skill, education, and experience will remain in demand (Rifkin, 1995; *The Economist*, 2014). Jobs lost in the other sectors will be gone forever, offset very little by the comparatively small number of jobs generated in the knowledge sector. And occupational retraining is believed to be no solution, since people in line for such retraining generally lack the necessary educational background on which to build the skills and information they would need to work in the knowledge sector.

These labor market trends are not apparent in the small business and skilled-trades spheres of occupational devotion. Newcomers will enter this kind of devotee work much as they have in the past, and no decrease appears on the horizon in the proportions so inspired. But substantial numbers of those who would like to break into some of the client-centered professions (e.g., accounting, *The Economist*, 2014) and all of the public-centered professions will find this career route increasingly difficult to follow. Frustrated thus in their quest for fulfilling work, what will these people do next? Having set their hearts on finding fulfillment while making a living do so, what will they do when the route is blocked? What is their future? Does this signal a return to the roots of occupational devotion, to serious leisure?

8

The Positive Quest for Fulfillment: Shadows

The preceding chapters have for the most part portrayed fulfillment as a positive goal and force in human life. Accent has been on the individual's developmental passage along the career path that makes this possible. The larger picture is more complex, however, for it can contain some negative or at least questionable shadows. We look at four of these: fulfillment as a never-ending search, community good, justification for selfishness, and basis for personal glory and individuation.

Fulfillment: Can participants get enough?[1]

Rephrased this question asks whether the serious pursuits are addictive, a possibility that was introduced in Chapter 5. Let it be clear from the outset that I have no intention in this section of trying to contribute to the vast scholarly and lay literature on addiction any thoughts about its causes. Addiction is presently an intellectual minefield, strewn with contradictory scientific definitions, wide-ranging lay opinion, numerous causal models, and an ample dose of emotional involvement in the entire question. Instead, my concern will be with whether it is valid to describe a powerful interest in a particular leisure or work activity as addictive, a common explanation today in some scientific and lay circles.

A definition of addiction for leisure studies

Aviel Goodman, a psychiatrist, developed a definition he believed fit both psychoactive substance abuse and pathological gambling. In his definition, which is broad enough to apply to leisure activities, he holds that

> essentially, addiction designates a process whereby a behavior, that can function both to produce pleasure and to provide escape from internal discomfort, is employed in a pattern characterized by (1) recurrent failure to control the behavior (powerlessness) and (2) continuation of the behavior despite significant negative consequences (unmanageability).
>
> (Goodman, 1990)

This statement refers to physical dependence on something, a condition where the addict suffers acute physiological symptoms when administration of it is stopped (e.g., psychoactive substance abuse). It also refers to psychological dependence. Here the addict feels that life is horribly dull when the effects of the drug or activity wear off; satisfaction and well-being are noticeably absent (e.g., pathological gambling; irresistible flow-based activities).

Addiction, substances, and casual leisure

Addiction as leisure is, on one level, clearly an oxymoron. This is the world of physical addiction. In it, addicts lose control over use of a drug on which they have become dependent (e.g., alcohol, nicotine, heroin, cocaine, hallucinogens). Although they initially take the drug frequently as leisure, later these people – now as addicts – have, in Goodman's terminology, grown powerless to control their addiction-generating activities as well as manage the consequences flowing from them. The unpleasant physical reactions resulting from any refusal to use the drug repeatedly drive these addicts back to active consumption. Such a scenario hardly sounds like leisure when defined as essentially uncoerced, freely chosen activity. Physically addicted people, when they feed their addiction, are not engaging in leisure.

Psychological dependence occupies a different world. Here there is no physical dependence – though some scholars still call it addiction – but rather an absence of a desired positive psychological state, such as tranquility, satiation, well-being, relaxation, or happiness. Thus, regular marijuana use is commonly believed to create psychological dependence in some people, as can use of prescription drugs like the barbiturates, amphetamines and tranquilizers. It is likewise for food addictions and addictions to sex and possibly exercise. A crucial difference between the psychologically addictive drugs, foods, and activities, on the one hand, and the drugs leading to a physical addiction, on the other, is that the first create a temporary *positive* mental state. By contrast, the second mainly avoid or temporarily eliminate a *negative* physical or psychological state (e.g., pain, fear, tremors, nausea). In both worlds a passing sense of well-being normally follows from consuming or engaging in the supposedly addictive substance or activity.

Dependence on a drug to produce a positive state of mind (as opposed to alleviating a negative state) has the same goal that many people seek in ordinary, non-drug-based leisure. But may we then say that positive dependence is leisure? The answer to this question depends on how coercive this drug dependency is. For example, do these users lack attractive alternative nonaddictive activities, as in consuming drugs to counteract boredom? Is there a genetic tendency toward using a particular drug? Does a person's lifestyle or certain past or present situations within it drive him or her, as it were, to one or more drugs? Are close associates of the user consuming the same drug or a similar one, creating thereby social pressure to conform to group interests? Affirmative answers to questions like these make it logically difficult to describe this kind of drug use as leisure. By the way, this relationship cries out for research and, ultimately, for a scale by which we can measure degrees of psychological dependence as it increasingly undermines the sense of leisure.

But, when the answers to questions like these are 'no', when such use is uncoerced, it would appear to be a leisure activity. More precisely it is, being hedonic, casual leisure, sought as relaxation or sensory stimulation or a combination of both.

Addiction, activity, and leisure

The label of addiction has also come to be applied by some professionals and many lay people to the psychological dependency thought to develop around such activities as work (workaholics), gambling (problem gamblers), shopping (shopaholics), television (TV addicts), religious practice (ritualists), mobile phone use (Leung, 2008), and surfing and gaming on the Internet (Li & Chung, 2006). People deeply attached to such activities may feel that, when denied an opportunity to engage in them, their psychological well-being is substantially threatened. Is not this feeling of threat a kind of withdrawal symptom?

To answer this question let us return to our definition: are these participants, these 'addicts', powerless to control their 'addiction', therefore continuing with the activity despite negative consequences? This could be true for the casual leisure activities mentioned in the preceding paragraph. But only if they are indeed uncontrollable, even in face of substantial negative consequences like threat of divorce, financial ruin, jail or a heavy fine, public ridicule, heart failure, and even death caused by certain eating disorders (e.g., bulimia, anorexia). If the so-called addict abandons his or her addictive activity because the costs for continuing them are perceived as too great, then this person has shown that with sufficient motivation the dependency can be controlled and managed. The habit has been broken (or never established) and any claim that it is an addiction shown to be invalid (see Johnson, 2009 for how this process works in so-called Internet addiction).

Given these rewards and distinguishing qualities, can serious leisure participants become addicted to their amateur, hobbyist or volunteer activity, activity that generates such a powerful personal return? The answer is, in general, 'no'. This conclusion can be explained by the condition that participation in any serious leisure activity is subject to a number of constraints. Six are mentioned here. The first is mental or physical fatigue, and sometimes both, felt after a lengthy session in the activity. The participant needs a rest. The second is institutional: work and nonwork obligations, including for some people familial obligations, force the enthusiast to spend time at nonleisure activities. A third is related to lifestyle: some people, even while holding a full-time job, are able to pursue more than one serious leisure activity during the same part of the year (e.g., tennis and playing in an orchestra; volunteering, collecting stamps, and skiing on weekends). Each activity constrains pursuit of the other(s). Moreover, some of these people may also get involved from time to time in a leisure project. Fourth, participation in some serious leisure is constrained by availability of coparticipants. For instance, SCUBA divers must descend with at least one other person, who may, however, be free for this activity only on a certain day of the week. Fifth, climatic conditions can constrain a person's leisure. Some these conditions are temporary, a snow or rain storm could force cancelation of a planned afternoon of snowmobiling or golfing, for example, as drought might dry up fishing opportunities or strong winds discourage sailing. But some climatic conditions are seasonal, such that snowmobiling can only be done in winter while sailing (on fresh water) is limited to times of the year when lakes are not frozen.

A sixth constraint is based on manageability. Serious leisure enthusiasts are highly enamored of what they do, such that they want to be able to return again and again to the activity. To the extent that engaging in it excessively risks injury, burnout, family or relational conflict, and other unpleasant repercussions that can constrain their involvement, many serious leisure participants are (however reluctantly) inclined to rein themselves in.

The controllability of serious leisure

Nevertheless, I have argued over the years (e.g., Stebbins, 2007b, pp. 17–18) that the desire to participate in a core amateur, hobbyist, or volunteer activity can become for some participants some of the time significantly *uncontrollable*. This is because it engenders in its practitioners the thirst to engage in the activity beyond the time or the money (if not both) available for it. I wish to underscore in the present chapter, however, that uncontrollability is a *tendency* not an inescapable compulsion or obsession. Furthermore, this tendency is often felt in ways having little to do directly with addiction, as in a desire to upgrade equipment or clothing or acquire more and more training or education.

Searching for flow

Considering the foregoing constraints to participation in serious leisure, it is difficult to see how it can, for the typical participant, be qualified as addiction. And that despite the passion that serious participants commonly express for their activities and the enthusiasm (as measured, for instance, in time, energy, and monetary costs) with which they go about them.

Nonetheless there are exceptions; some people defy these constraints suggesting thereby that they are addicted to, or dependent on, their serious leisure. Consider Régine Cavagnoud, French world champion in alpine skiing, who died in a collision with a ski coach while hurtling down a slope in the Alps.

Many times previously Miss Cavagnoud had been badly injured on the slopes while pushing herself to her natural constraints, and probably beyond, in her drive to become a world champion.... Miss Cavagnoud did feel fear. Considering the risks involved, there have been relatively few deaths on the slopes.... But many skiers are badly injured. Miss Cavagnoud dreaded ending up in a wheelchair. But even more, she said, she dreaded doing badly.

(*The Economist*, 2001)

Giddens (1992, pp. 70–74) wrote about similar 'characteristics of addiction' leading to high-risk leisure, when discussing ecstatic experience, the fix gained from having it and, thereby, being 'transported to another world' beyond everyday life. The vast majority of high-risk leisure participants (e.g., alpine skiers, bicycle racers, and para-gliders) are content with the level of flow (Csikszentmihalyi, 1990) experienced from doing their activity and avoid situations where they lack full control of and competence in the activity. Not so with a minority of them who seem hooked on the strong, positive, emotional, and physiological feelings that come with going over the top edge of their control and competence. Some say they are motivated by an 'adrenalin rush'. While this would be abhorrent to the majority, it becomes for this minority as it did for Ms Cavagnoud an addictive magnetism, accompanying fear notwithstanding.

According to Goodman's definition, addiction results from searching for pleasure as a remedy for internal discomfort. This combined interest in finding pleasure while alleviating discomfort, the concept of addiction suggests, is frequent and recurring. Thus, once rested addicted skiers and bicycle racers would be irresistibly and recurrently drawn to the slopes and roads, free of the constraints mentioned earlier. And, presumably, if their activity is seasonal, they would be driven to find an equally exciting counterpart during the off-season. The same may be said for actors, jazz musicians, ballet dancers, and some others in the performing arts. They simply cannot get enough of expressing their talent and feeling the flow it generates and who, as addicts, have abandoned all allegiance to these constraints. Still, such hyperenthusiasts are comparatively uncommon.

Searching for success and fulfillment

The drive for success and fulfillment in any field of work or leisure can be heavily time-consuming, suggesting to some people that addiction is the cause of activity this intense. Where success is achieved through strongly felt flow experiences and the constraints of participation are ignored, as can happen in playing jazz or engaging in alpine skiing, for example, addiction could conceivably be an outcome. But, when success is reached in activities offering only weak flow, or none at all, the label of addiction seems far-fetched, implausible. Meanwhile, more empirically valid and profound explanations for such behavior exist. They include the list of rewards presented earlier and the six qualities of the serious pursuits. Furthermore, these observations call into question whether the supposed workaholic is really an addict, as some writers have claimed (see Chapter 6).

The drive for success and fulfillment does not mean that the behavior leading to it is uncontrollable, as true addictions are. Rather the successful person in leisure or work knows well what it takes to succeed and, with a strong sense of control and personal competence, has set out to reach this goal. Such people *are* in reasonable control of an unfolding career personally designed to achieve identifiable rewards. In other words, the drive for success is fired by a variety of positive activities. By contrast addiction itself, as defined in this article, is negative – an unpleasant state – to which the addiction-related behavior brings only temporary relief. This hardly sounds like an antecedent to success in the multitude of activities in which people aspire to achieve this goal.

Selfishness and the search for fulfillment

It is at the point of choosing leisure activities and allocating time to pursuing them that selfishness can manifest itself. Selfishness is an act of a self-seeker judged as selfish by the victim of that act (Stebbins, 1995). When we define an act as selfish, we make an imputation. This imputation is most commonly hurled at perceived self-seekers by their victims, where the self-seekers are felt to demonstrate a concern for their own welfare or advantage at the expense of or in disregard for those victims. The central thread running in the fabric of selfishness is exploitative unfairness – a kind of personal favoritism infecting one's everyday affairs.

Leisure activities, especially the serious ones, have – as we have just seen – magnetic pull. This pull can be so strong that, at times, participants may be accused of being selfish in their use of time and perhaps money. These commodities are seen by those claiming selfishness as rightfully theirs. Such accusations may be denied by the participant thus 'charged', leading most of the time to acrimonious argument. There is evidence in culture (e.g., search on Google for 'golf widow', 'baseball widow', 'theater widow') and in research (see Stebbins, 1995), both showing that relationships can be severely strained by leisure selfishness.

Such contretemps severely reduce the positiveness that is the hallmark of leisure. Thus planning well for leisure requires participants to keep selfishness at bay. One route to this goal is to include where possible those who would be adversely affected by an overstrong commitment to a particular activity. So, get them hooked on traveling, collecting, hiking, bridge, or whatever one's passion. If they have little interest in it, perhaps there is a parallel activity that appeals. She loves to hike; he has no taste for it, but does love to assemble her photos from the outback into slide shows or for posting them online. He loves to travel; her medical conditions prevent this, but she reads voraciously on the regions he visits, thereby being able to supply him with a rich historical, cultural, and geographical background of them.

Is the fulfillment career good for society?

Something as individual and personal as a fulfillment career might, at first blush, appear irrelevant to the larger society. Still, on numerous occasions, serious leisure enthusiasts do contribute significantly to the social and cultural enrichment of their local community. This kind of community involvement is evident when, for example, the town's civic orchestra provides it every three or four months with a concert of classical music or the local astronomy society offers an annual 'star night' during which the public may observe the heavens using the telescopes of club members. And model railroaders in the area sometimes mount for popular consumption exhibitions of the fruits of their hobby. Lyons and Dionigi (2007) found, in a study of older Australian adults in Masters sports, that, through their participation, they feel a sense of 'giving something back' to the community. Though most thinkers in the area fail to conceive of these activities as voluntary action, they certainly fit the definition of such action, as do the activities discussed in the next paragraph. Furthermore, Hemingway (1999) and Reid (1995) have argued that, when considering leisure's contribution to community, it is important to distinguish between different kinds of activities. The examples above – all of them serious leisure – illustrate contributions quite distinct from those made through casual or project-based forms.

A broader sort of community involvement (sometimes also carried out on a regional or societal level) comes from pursuing volunteer activities, which may be enacted as serious, casual, or project-based leisure. This is the most common conception of 'community involvement', which is often discussed as 'civil labor'. It, too, is voluntary action, although a type that finds members of a local community participating together as volunteers in nonprofit groups or other community activities. On this level, a principal intention is to improve community life. Civil labor, which is broadly synonymous with community involvement, differs mainly in emphasis; it is on human activity devoted to unpaid renewal and expansion of social capital (Rojek, 2002, p. 21). Beck (2000, p. 125) says that civil labor comprises housework, family work, club work, and volunteer work. This is an extremely general conception, however, since it includes the area of unpaid work, the domain of nonwork obligation.

Rojek (2002, pp. 26–27) argues that, for the most part, civil labor consists of the community contribution made by amateurs, hobbyists, and career volunteers when they pursue their serious leisure. This is precisely what Leadbeater and Miller (2004) had in mind in their book about how amateurs in various fields are shaping the 21st-century economy and society in the West. Helft (2007) offers a concrete example in an article about amateur cartographers, who using simple Internet tools, are reshaping online map services and offering viewers far more detail of many more geographic sites than heretofore. Along these same lines, Levine (2007) holds that democracy depends on citizen participation, and that too many of today's young Americans lack the skills needed for this.

Civil labor, however conceived of, generates 'social capital', defined here, following Putnam (2000, p. 19), as the links among individuals manifested in social networks, trustworthiness, acts motivated by the norm of reciprocity, and the like that develop in a community or larger society. The term is an analogy to the concepts of human capital and physical capital (e.g., financial resources, natural resources); it emphasizes that human groups of all kinds also benefit from and advance their interests according to the salutary interrelations of their members. Community involvement also generates social capital, but as noted earlier, it includes amateur and hobbyist activities, where this result, though it occurs, is not their primary purpose.

Clearly, to be community involvement, leisure must be collective in some manner; the reclusive hobbies (e.g., liberal arts, some amateur piano and guitar), for example, fail to qualify. Furthermore, when it comes to social capital, as opposed to civil labor and community involvement, I see no case for privileging any of the three forms of leisure as the principal or most important way of generating the former. What is important is that people come together in voluntary action, as motivated by voluntary altruism, doing so long enough to learn something about one another, learn to trust one another (where experience warrants), develop 'other-regarding' or altruistic love for one another (Jeffries et al., 2006), and for these reasons become willing to continue their interaction. True, many forms of serious leisure encourage sustained contact capable of fostering such learning, as seen in routine participation in many volunteer emergency services, hobbyist clubs, and arts and sports groups. Project leisure can also be a source of social capital, though here, such capital is of more limited scope than that generated through enduring serious leisure activities. As for casual leisure volunteering, it may be of short or long term.

Risky leisure for glory and individuality

One possible, dramatic outcome of the fulfillment career is individualization of the participant, whereby this person achieves an uncommon distinctiveness in a serious pursuit. In fact, individuality may be realized in casual and project-based leisure, but since fulfillment careers root primarily in the serious pursuits, I will confine myself to the latter (Cohen-Gewerc & Stebbins, 2013). It is in the quest for glory and individuality in one of those pursuits that selfishness can reach its extreme expression.

Be they highly committed enthusiasts – even addicts – seekers of glory in the extreme sports and hobbies may be accused of being selfish by intimates who will suffer mightily with what the latter see as probable death or serious injury of the former. In these circumstances, the intimates may conclude, sooner or later, that the enthusiast is far more enamored of the core leisure activity and its glory than of them. When a participant, seemingly out of control, takes on too much of the activity or too much risk in doing it, imputations of selfishness from certain important others (whether overtly made or covertly held) are surely just around the corner.

Individuated performance in this kind of serious leisure is heady stuff, though chiefly for the participant. It is easy to see how in searching for distinctiveness such people might engage in some selfish acts. Still, at least in some serious activities, individuated involvement raises some prickly questions. Do its lofty ends – for example, providing the community in remarkable ways with amateur theater, volunteering for an extraordinary number of hours for the Salvation Army, or providing the same lengthy service for the Olympic Games – justify the selfish means by which they are sometimes reached?

Moreover, some enthusiasts who go in for high-risk activity are literally paid by a sponsor to engage in it. The latter is hoping to sensationally promote a product. There is also the possibility of further remuneration from the feat gained through public speaking engagements or a contracted book or article. The most celebrated might even be recognized in *Guinness World Records*.[2] A number of popular books glorify taking intentional high risk in nature, thereby contributing disproportionately to the popular image that the hobbies in question are inherently hazardous (e.g., Sebastian Junger, *The Perfect Storm* [1999]; Jonathan Shay, *Achilles in Viet Nam* [1995]). Still, self-fulfillment for glory and individuation is not the usual goal of the fulfillment career, where the core activities of the serious pursuit have enormous intrinsic appeal, a vast reward of its own.

Conclusions

Ashley Montagu (Anglo-American anthropologist and humanist) once observed that 'by virtue of being born to humanity, every human being has a right to the development and fulfillment of his potentialities as a human being'. The fulfillment career offers a clear, though often demanding, path to realizing this right. The path has its rough sections. Yet, many (possibly most) travelers on this route avoid the most difficult of these. They avoid the poignant repercussions of selfishness, eschew glory through individuality, and remain outside the zone of addictive noncontrol. They are the ones who experience a deep sense of well-being, unadulterated by possible disastrous accidents (risky leisure), interpersonal bitterness (selfishness), and uncontrollable pursuit of the activity (addiction).

A major challenge facing our world in the 21st century is how to enable and encourage more people everywhere to follow this path and thereby experience the fulfillment and well-being available at trail's end. To help meet this challenge, we will need the fruits of leisure education (gained through adult education, formal instruction in schools, self-directed learning, and so on; see Dieser, 2013). Long brushed aside as relatively trivial compared with, for example, education for work or for life skills, education for leisure does provide an effective compass for guiding people toward a career in the serious pursuits. Aided thus we will be able to devote our energy to ensuring the unique and vital contributions to the human existence that fulfillment can make.

Notes

1 The Serious Leisure Perspective

1. Presented here as most recently set out in Stebbins (2012a).

2 Starting a Fulfillment Career

1. This conceptualization of play is that of Johan Huizinger (1955).
2. *Amator* is the Latin base for 'amateur', or lover of something. In this broad sense of lover, all people in the serious pursuits are *amators* of their core activities.
3. The psychology of positive interest takes us in this direction, which, however, revolves around interest as a general emotion rather than interest in a particular leisure activity (see Fredrickson, 1998).
4. For a rich answer to why I like to write, see http://www.inkpunks .com/2012/05/12/why-do-we-write/. For one on why I like to paint, see http://wanderingmist.com/inspiration/why-do-we-paint/. Both retrieved April 28, 2013.
5. See also Lindesmith, Strauss, and Denzin (1991) and Hewitt (1991).
6. Some support for these observations is presented in Stebbins (1992, pp. 72–73).
7. The concept of scientist as entrepreneur being developed here is different from that of entrepreneurial scientist, or someone who, for personal or institutional profit, turns a scholarly product into a saleable item (see Etzkowitz, 1989).

3 Amateurism as a Route to Fulfillment

1. Solo acts, or shows, are given in both dance and theater, even though most performances in these arts involve two or more dancers or actors. This section treats only of collective fine art.
2. Early amateurs in jazz and dance music commonly perform gratis. Later, some of them may demand a fee for their services, but still fail to earn enough to become dependent on such payment. Professionals are paid and dependent on that remuneration but, for charitable reasons, they are usually willing to play occasionally for no pay.
3. Stage business is any activity that is not in the script, but performed by an actor for dramatic effect.
4. The five basic ballet positions are shown in http://dance.about.com/od/ typesofdance/p/Ballet.htm (retrieved 30 March 2013).

5. 'Nutcracker Performances' are presentations of Tchaikovsky's Nutcracker Suite, given primarily in December (often far) away from America's main ballet centers. Here senior members of the corps de ballet may get a rare opportunity to dance a principal role, the stars of the company being uninterested in such distant work.

6. Lack of space prevents a detailed description of the skills, knowledge, and experience that amateurs must acquire in the various individual arts. But, as in the collective arts, participants must persevere, which because these acquisitions are substantial, requires considerable effort.

7. Craig adapted the career framework set out in this book to the career line typical of her sample of poets.

8. See Amazon.com for lists of books for adults who want to work with children in these crafts.

9. The exceptions to this generalization fall primarily under the heading of folk art. The folk music mentioned in the next paragraph is of the entertainment variety presented in (often) colorful urban venues. It differs from the native or backcountry art performed in certain isolated areas of North America and various societies outside the West.

10. Country dance has a professional wing in which participants dance the waltz, two-step, triple-two, and other dances. See http://www .UCWDCworlds.com (retrieved 9 May 2013).

11. Kayaking and alpine skiing need not be competitive, need not be a sport. Instead, they may be pursued as hobbies, wherein the challenge faced is what nature presents. On nature challenge activities, see Davidson and Stebbins (2011).

12. These sources of learning for bodybuilding are set out in detail in Klein (1993, pp. 69–79).

13. In fact, most professionals in both the team and the individual sports are rather modestly remunerated, a condition that can contribute to parental anxiety. According to the U.S. Bureau of Labor Statistics the annual mean wage for 'athletes and sports competitors' in May 2012 was $75,760 (http://www.bls.gov/oes/current/oes_nat.htm#27 -0000, retrieved 13 April 2013).

14. This research is reported in Stebbins (1979; 1980; 1981; 1982), which are referenced in www.seriousleisure.net/Bibliography/Amateurs.

15. This is not an attempt to liken amateur scientists to tradesmen. In everyday usage, these three terms are applied to any field where extensive knowledge and ability must be developed before independent practice is possible (see Stebbins, 1980).

16. These three concepts are further discussed in Stebbins (1980).

17. My interviews suggest that the first journal article or two are regarded as turning points for avocational scientists.

18. All amateurs, apprentices included, are aware of the possibility of accidentally discovering something new. But even apprentices observe or do fieldwork chiefly for other reasons, realizing how rare such discoveries are.

19. Routier (2013) interviewed a sample of physically active hobbyists who abandoned their activities because of this contingency and some of the others discussed in this section.

4 Finding Fulfillment in a Hobby

1. Note that these collectors are not gatherers. Gathering refers to acquiring a resource for subsequent use in making something. Thus, some people gather driftwood for sculpturing or home decoration. Others gather beach pebbles, sea shells, or beach glass (glass washed up on shore), with which, for example, they assemble mosaics or bottled decorations or mount individual pieces for display. Gatherers are hobbyists of the maker and tinkering variety; they are neither collectors nor casual leisure accumulators (Davidson & Stebbins, 2011, p. 136).
2. King (2001) discusses the extensive 'social outreach' of quilting.
3. Barbershop singing is the only folk art on which we have any career-related data (Stebbins, 1996). Given this general lack of research on careers in folk art, this kind of leisure will not be considered further here.
4. To the extent that spelunkers engage in speleology, the scientific exploration and study of caves and other underground features, they are amateur scientists rather than hobbyist activity participants.
5. Mountain climbing is an exception to this observation, for climbers may be intensely aware of 'kinesthetic sensations' (Mitchell, Jr, 1983, p. 166).
6. There is also no small number of body-centered activities of the casual leisure variety, among them walking, popular dance, and, when defined as enjoyable, jogging.
7. Bartram (2001) found that white-water kayakers commonly get their start by taking a course, though a smaller number of them learn informally from friends or on their own with rental equipment. She examined all five stages of the hobbyist career of her sample.
8. Cheng and Tsaur (2012) have examined the six qualities of serious leisure among wave surfers.
9. Hamilton (1979) discusses the prominence rock climbers gain from making 'first ascents'.
10. Collison and Hockey (2007) studied runners' identities, while Dilley and Scraton (2010) examined those of female mountain climbers.
11. Since some people make money playing bridge, it is in order to ask whether bridge should be classified as an amateur activity. But according to Holtz (1975), the title 'professional bridge player' is a misnomer. She argues that the people who play bridge for money do so as secretly paid partners in a leisure activity officially held to be strictly amateur.
12. The intellectually oriented followers of politics who are committed to a certain political party or doctrine still spend a significant amount of time (and possibly money), informing themselves widely in this area. To be a hobbyist here, a person must pursue a broad knowledge and understanding; he or she must do more than merely proclaim, however, fervently such and such a political stripe.
13. On the skills of reading, see Prose (2009) and Stebbins (2013b, pp. 8–9).
14. This transition is briefly mentioned in Chapter 1, with a deeper discussion being available in Stebbins (1979, pp. 19–22).

5 Fulfilling Careers in Volunteering

1. Corporate philanthropy is not germane to this discussion.
2. It is possible to dabble in horticulture, such as sticking a seed in some dirt to see what happens. But it is debatable whether this dabbling leads to a serious interest in gardening and, for some, on to floral volunteering of one variety or another.
3. Insects in general fail to attract volunteers, even while the Internet reveals considerable concern for honeybees and butterflies. Expressing this concern as a leisure activity primarily occurs as a hobbyist pursuit, which includes building and maintaining horticultural habitats that foster their survival. Volunteering to help with the social movement whose mission is to save the bees or the butterflies falls under the rubric of environmental volunteering (see the next section).
4. There are other kinds of marginal volunteering, which are not treated here. These include receiving advantageous tax deductions for volunteer service, in-kind or monetary payments that significantly augment one's livelihood, and corporate and educational volunteering demanded of participants in accordance with work place goals (e.g., corporate social responsibility programs) or course requirements.

6 Professional Devotee Work

1. As a correction to this situation, Etsy, an eBay-style Internet outlet for small-scale sellers of art and craft, has been successful in marketing creative, noncommercial works where brick-and-mortar stores have had to struggle (www.etsy.com).
2. The Fifteen-Year Project, carried out by the author, was summarized in Stebbins (1992). It consisted of eight exploratory field studies of amateurs and professionals in art (theater and classical music), sport (baseball and Canadian football), science (archaeology and astronomy), and entertainment (magic and stand-up comedy). The studies were conducted between 1973 and 1990.
3. This is not to deny that individual workers in a variety of occupations (e.g., trade, managerial, proprietary, clerical, political) sometimes approach their work with the spirit just described for professionals. These individuals are not typical of their occupation, however, and their exceptional spirit therefore fails to constitute part of its subculture.

7 Hobbyist and Volunteer Devotee Work

1. Are these service specialists another variety of trades-worker, albeit one without significant physical skills? It appears not. The following definition by the Social Security Administration (Government of

the United States) suggests that these workers are actually semiskilled. Semiskilled is

> work which needs some skills but does not require doing the more complex work duties. Semi-skilled jobs may require alertness and close attention to watching machine processes; or inspecting, testing or otherwise looking for irregularities; or tending or guarding equipment, property, materials, or persons against loss, damage or injury; or other types of activities which are similarly less complex than skilled work, but more complex than unskilled work.
>
> (http://www.myattorneyhome.com/Glossary/semi-skilled-work, retrieved January 22, 2014)

2. Gardening is a possible exception. One might plant a seed simply to see how it will grow. But even here there is intentionality: to produce a plant. Dabbling is intrinsically motivated, to enjoy the experience of the moment, in this instance planting the seed and imagining its germination.
3. Preference for the title of trade, technical, or vocational seems to vary by country (*Encyclopedia Britannica*, 2014, online edition).

8   The Positive Quest for Fulfillment: Shadows

1. This section is taken from Stebbins (2010).
2. Most of the time, however, *Guinness World Records* distinctions celebrate achievements in casual or project-based leisure such as how many pizzas or hot dogs are consumed in a specified period of time.

References

Adler, J. (1975). Innovative art and obsolescent artists. *Social Research*, 42, 360–78.

Adler, P., & Adler, P. (1991). *Backboards and blackboards: College athletes and role engulfment*. New York: Columbia University Press.

Allison, M.T., & Meyer, C. (1988). Career problems and retirement of elite athletes: The female tennis player. *Sociology of Sport Journal*, 5, 212–22.

Altheide, D.L., & Snow, R.P. (1991). *Media worlds in the postjournalism era*. Hawthorne, NY: Aldine de Gruyter.

Amsden, B., & McEntee, J. (2011). Agrileisure: Re-imagining the relationship between agriculture, leisure and social change. *Leisure/Loisir*, 35, 37–48.

Back, K.W. (1981). Small groups. In M. Rosenberg & R.H. Turner (Eds.), *Social psychology* (pp. 320–43). New York: Basic Books.

Backlund, E.A., & Kuentzel, W.F. (2013). Beyond progression in specialization research: Leisure capital and participation change. *Leisure Sciences*, 35, 293–99.

Baldwin, C.K., & Norris, P.A. (1999). Exploring the dimensions of serious leisure: Love me – love my dog. *Journal of Leisure Research*, 31, 1–17.

Ball, D.W. (1976). Failure in sport. *American Sociological Review*, 41, 726–39.

Bartram, S.A. (2001). Serious leisure careers among whitewater kayakers: A feminist perspective. *World Leisure Journal*, 43(2), 4–11.

Basirico, L.A. (1986). The art and craft fair. *Qualitative Sociology*, 9, 339–53.

Beamish, R. (1982). Sport and the logic of capitalism. In H. Cantelon & R. Gruneau (Eds.), *Sport, culture, and the modern state* (pp. 141–97). Toronto: University of Toronto Press.

Beck, U. (2000). *The brave new world of work,* trans. by P. Camiller. New York: Polity Press.

Becker, H.S. (1982). *Art worlds*. Berkeley, CA: University of California Press.

Belk, R. (2004). Collecting. In G.S. Cross (Ed.), *Encyclopedia of recreation and leisure in America* (pp. 192–99). New York: Thompson Gale.

Booth, W. (1999). *For the love of it: Amateuring and its rivals*. Chicago, IL: University of Chicago Press.

Borden, S. (2013). Pickup soccer in Brazil has an allure all its own. *New York Times*, 16 October (online edition).

Borns, B. (1987). *Comic lives: Inside the world of American stand-up comedy*. New York: Simon & Schuster.

Braverman, H. (1974). *Labor and monopoly capital: The degradation of work in the twentieth century*. New York: Monthly Review Press.

Bryan, H. (1977). Leisure value systems and recreational specialization: The case of trout fishermen. *Journal of Leisure Research*, 9, 174–87.

Carrier, R. (1995). What price culture? *The Financial Post*, 28 October, 23.

Cheng, T.-M., & Tsaur, S.-H. (2012). The relationship between serious leisure characteristics and recreation involvement: A case study of Taiwan's surfing activities. *Leisure Studies*, 31, 53–68.

Chevalier, V., Le Mancq, F., & Simonet, M. (2011). Amateurs, bénévoles et professionnelles: Analyse des carrières et usages des statuts. In A. Degenne, C. Marry, & S. Moulin (Eds.), *Les catégories sociales et leurs frontières* (pp. 147–87). Québec, QC: Les Presses de l'Université Laval.

Coakley, J. (1992). Burnout among adolescent athletes: A personal failure or social problem? *Sociology of Sport Journal*, 9, 271–85.

Coakley, J. (2001). *Sport in society: Issues and controversies*, 7th ed. New York: McGraw-Hill.

Cohen-Gewerc, E., & Stebbins, R.A. (2013). *Serious leisure and individuality*. Montreal, QC & Kingston, ON: McGill-Queens University Press.

Collinson, J. A., & Hockey, J. (2007). 'Working out' identity: Distance runners and the management of disrupted identity. *Leisure Studies*, 26, 381–98.

Connor, J. (2009). The athlete as widget: How exploitation explains elite sport. *Sport in Society: Cultures, Commerce, Media, Politics*, 12(10), 1369–77.

Cotter, H. (2014). Holland Cotter looks at money in art. *New York Times*, 17 January (online edition).

Craig, A. (2006). *The practice of poetry: Identity, community and subculture*. Doctoral thesis, Department of Sociology, New York University.

Craig, A. (2007). Practicing poetry: A career without a job. In C. Calhoun & R. Sennett (Eds.), *Practicing culture (taking culture seriously)*, pp. 35–56. New York: Routledge.

Csikszentmihalyi, M. (1990). *Flow: The psychology of optimal experience*. New York, NY: Harper & Row.

Curtis, J., & Ennis, R. (1988). Negative consequences of leaving competitive sport? Comparative findings for former elite-level hockey players. *Sociology of Sport Journal*, 5, 87–106.

Davidson, L., & Stebbins, R.A. (2011). *Serious leisure and nature: Sustainable consumption in the outdoors*. Houndmills, UK: Palgrave Macmillan.

Derom, I., & Taks, M. (2011). Participants' experiences in two types of sporting events: A quest for evidence of the SL-CL continuum. *Journal of Leisure Research*, 43, 383–402.

Diep, F. (2011). Amateur cartographers map local 'food desert.' *Scientific American*, 28 February (online edition).

Dieser, R. (2013). *Leisure education: A person-centered, system-directed, and social policy Perspective*. Urbana, IL: Sagamore.

Dilley, R.E., & Scraton, S.J. (2010). Women, climbing and serious leisure. *Leisure Studies*, 29, 125–41.

Dirom, J. (2014). City's entrepreneurs kick-start success with crowd funding. *Calgary Herald*, 7 February, B1.

Dubin, R. (1992). *Central life interests: Creative individualism in a complex world*. New Brunswick, NJ: Transaction.

The Economist. (2001). Régine Cavagnoud, 17 November, 82.

The Economist. (2004). A great wall of waste (Special report on China's environment), 21 August, 55–7.

The Economist. (2005). Up off the Couch, 22 October, 35.

The Economist. (2010). Doctoral degrees: The disposable academic, 16 December, Online edition.

The Economist. (2013a). Busking it, 12 October, 41.

The Economist. (2013b). Ultimate recognition, 5 October, 68.

The Economist. (2014). The onrushing wave, 18 January, 24–8.

Encyclopedia Britannica. (2014). Vocational education (online edition).

Etzkowitz, H. (1989). Entrepreneurial science in the academy: A case of the transformation of norms. *Social Problems*, 36, 14–29.

Farmer, J. (2012). Leisure in living local through food and farming. *Leisure Sciences*, 34, 490–95.

Faulkner, R.R. (1973). Career concerns and mobility motivations of orchestra musicians. *Sociological Quarterly*, 14, 334–49.

Faulkner, R.R. (1975). Coming of age in organizations: A comparative study of career contingencies of musicians and hockey players. In D.W. Ball & J. Loy (Eds.), *Sport and social order* (pp. 521–58). Reading, MA: Addison-Wesley.

Federico, R.C. (1974). Recruitment, training, and performance: The case of ballet. In P.L. Stewart & M.G. Cantor (Eds.), *Varieties of work experience*. New York: Wiley.

Fine, G.A. (1983). *Shared fantasy: Role-playing games as social worlds.* Chicago: University of Chicago Press.

Fine, G.A. (1989). Mobilizing fun: Provisioning resources in leisure worlds. *Sociology of Sport Journal*, 6, 319–34.

Fine, G.A. (1998). *Morel tales: The culture of mushrooming.* Cambridge, MA: Harvard University Press.

Florida, R. (2014). *The rise of the creative class – Revisited*, revised and expanded. New York: Basic Books.

Fredrickson, B.L. (1998). What good are positive emotions? *Review of General Psychology*, 2, 300–19.

Friedman, N.L. (1990). The Hollywood actor: Occupational culture, career, and adaptation in a buyers' market industry. In H.Z. Lopata (Ed.), *Current research on occupations and professions*. Greenwich, CT: JAI.

Gage III, R., & Thapa, B. (2012). Volunteer motivations and constraints among college students: Analysis of the volunteer function inventory and leisure constraints models. *Nonprofit and Voluntary Sector Quarterly*, 41, 405–30.

Gelber, S.L. (1992). Free market metaphor: The historical dynamics of stamp collecting. *Comparative Studies in Society and History*, 34, 742–67.

Gerson, J. (2010). Video games keep kids fit. *Calgary Herald*, 8 December, B1.

Getz, D., & Andersson, T.D. (2010). The event-tourist career trajectory: A study of high-involvement amateur distance runners. *Scandinavian Journal of Hospitality and Tourism*, 10, 468–91.

Gibbons, J.A. (1979). Artists and dealers: A note on the role of the art dealer in the legitimization of culture. In J. Zuzanek (Ed.), *Social research and cultural policy*. Waterloo, ON: Otium Publications, University of Waterloo Press.

Giddens, A. (1992). *The transformation of intimacy: Sexuality, love & eroticism in modern societies*. Cambridge, UK: Polity.

Goffman, E. (1961). *Asylums: Essays on the social situation of mental patients and other inmates*. Garden City, NY: Doubleday.

Goodman, A. (1990). Addiction: Definition and implications. *British Journal of Addiction*, 85, 1403–08.

Green, B., & Chalip, L. (2004). Paths to volunteer commitment: Lessons from the Sydney Olympic games. In R.A. Stebbins & M. Graham (Eds.), *Volunteering as leisure/leisure as volunteering: An international assessment* (pp. 49–68). Wallingford, UK: CABI.

Greendorfer, S.L., & Blinde, E.M. (1987). 'Retirement' from intercollegiate sports. In A. Yiannakis, T.D. McIntyre, M.J. Melnick & D.P. Hart (Eds.), *Sport sociology*, 3rd ed. Dubuque, IA: Kendall/Hunt.

Gutting, G. (2013). The real humanities crisis. *New York Times*, 30 November (online edition).

Habenstein, R.W. (1962). Sociology of occupations: The case of the American funeral director. In A.M. Rose (Ed.), *Human behavior and social processes* (pp. 225–46). Boston, MA: Houghton Mifflin.

Hanna, J.L. (1988). *Dance, sex, and gender*. Chicago, IL: University of Chicago Press.

Hamilton, L.C. (1979). Modern American rock climbing. *Pacific Sociological Review*, 22, 285–308.

Harper, D. (2007). Work and occupations. In C.D. Bryant & D.L. Peck (Eds.), *21st century sociology: A reference handbook* (pp. 218–26). Thousand Oaks, CA: Sage.

Harper, S.J. (2013). The tyranny of the billable hour. *New York Times*, 28 March (online edition).

Hastings, D.W., Kurth, S.B., & Schloder, M. (1996). Work routines in the serious leisure career of Canadian and U.S. Masters swimmers. *Avanté*, 2, 73–92.

Hearle, Rudolf K., Jr. (1975). Career patterns and career contingencies of professional baseball players. In D.W. Ball & J.W. Loy (Eds.), *Sport and social order* (pp. 457–520). Reading, MA: Addison-Wesley.

Helft, M. (2007). With tools on Web, amateurs reshape mapmaking. *New York Times*, 27 July (online edition).

Hemingway, J.L. (1999). Leisure, social capital, and democratic citizenship. *Journal of Leisure Research*, 31, 150–65.

Heuser, L. (2005). We're not too old to play sports: The career of women lawn bowlers. *Leisure Studies*, 24, 45–60.

Holmes, K. (2001). The motivation and retention of front-house volunteers at museum and heritage attractions. In M. Graham & M. Foley (Eds.), *Leisure volunteering: Marginal or inclusive?* (pp. 95–110). Eastbourne, UK: Leisure Studies Association, LSA Publication No. 75.

Holmes, K. (2006). Volunteering, obligation, and serious leisure. In S. Elkington, I. Jones, & L. Lawrence (Eds.), *Serious leisure: Extensions and applications* (pp. 5–18). Eastbourne, UK: Leisure Studies Association, LSA Publication No. 95.

Holtz, J.A. (1975). The 'professional' duplicate bridge player. *Urban Life*, 4, 131–48.

Houlston, D.R. (1982). The occupational mobility of professional athletes. *International Review of Sport Sociology*, 17(2), 15–28.

Hughes, E.C. (1937). Institutional office and the person. *American Journal of Sociology*, 43, 404–13.

Huizinger J. (1955). *Homo ludens: A study of the play element in culture*. Boston: Beacon, 1955.

Hutchinson, S.L., & Kleiber, D.A. (2005). Gifts of the ordinary: Casual leisure's contributions to health and well-being. *World Leisure Journal*, 47(3), 2–16.

Jeffries, V., Johnston, B.V., Nichols, L.T., Oliner, S.P., Tiryakian, E., & Weinstein, J. (2006). Altruism and social solidarity: Envisioning a field of specialization. *American Sociologist*, 37(3), 67–83.

Johnson, N.F. (2009). *The multiplicities of internet addiction: The misrecognition of leisure and learning*. Burlington, VT: Ashgate.

Kadlcik, J., & Flemr, L. (2008). Athletic career termination model in the Czech Republic: A qualitative exploration. *International Review for the Sociology of Sport*, 43, 251–69.

Kalleberg, A.L. (2007). *The mismatched worker*. New York: W.W. Norton.

Karp, D.A. (1989). The social construction of retirement among professionals. *The Gerontologist*, 29, 750–60.

Kennelly, M., Moyle, B., & Lamont, M. (2013). Constraint negotiation in serious leisure: A study of amateur triathletes. *Journal of Leisure Research*, 45, 466–84.

King, F.L. (2001). Social dynamics of quilting. *World Leisure Journal*, 43(2), 26–9.

Kleiber, D.A. (2000). The neglect of relaxation. *Journal of Leisure Research*, 32, 82–86.

Kleiber, D., Greendorfer, S., Blinde, E., & Samdahl, D. (1987). Quality of exit from university sports and life satisfaction in early adulthood. *Sociology of Sport Journal*, 4, 28–36.

Klein, A.M. (1993). *Little big men: Bodybuilding subculture and gender construction*. Albany, NY: State University of New York Press.

Kutner, N.G. (1983). The touring tennis player. In I.H. Simpson & R.L. Simpson (Eds.), *Research in the sociology of work*. Greenwich, CT: JAI.

Larkin, C. (Ed.) (1999). *The Virgin encyclopedia of jazz*. London: Virgin Books.

Leadbeater, C., & Miller, P. (2004). *The pro-am revolution: How enthusiasts are changing our economy and society*. London, UK: Demos.

Leakey, R., & Morell, V. (2001). *Wildlife wars: My fight to save Africa's natural treasures*. New York: St. Martins.

Leung, L. (2008) Linking psychological attributes to addiction and improper use of the mobile phone among adolescents in Hong Kong. *Journal of Children and Media*, 2(2), 93–113.

Levine, P. (2007). *The future of democracy: Developing the next generation of American citizens*. Medford, MA: Tufts University Press.

Levy, E. (1989). The choice of acting as a profession. In A.W. Foster & J.R. Blau (Eds.), *Art and society*. Albany, NY: State University of New York Press.

Lewis, J., Patterson, I., & Pegg, S. (2013). The serious leisure career hierarchy of Australian motorcycle road racers. *World Leisure Journal*, 55(2), 179–92.

Li, S.-M., & Chung, T.-M. (2006). Internet function and internet addictive behaviour. *Computers in Human Behaviour*, 22(6), 1067–71.

Lindesmith, A.R., Strauss, A.L., & Denzin, N.K. (1991). *Social psychology*, 7th ed. Englewood Cliffs, NJ: Prentice-Hall.

Lyons, K., & Dionigi, R. (2007). Transcending emotional community: A qualitative examination of older adults and Masters' sports participation. *Leisure Sciences*, 29, 375–89.

Mah, B. (2012). Buyout from province paid for brewing startup. *Calgary Herald*, Monday, 14 May, B3.

Mahoney, M.J. (1976). *Scientist as subject: The psychological imperative*. Cambridge, MA: Ballinger.

Major, W.F. (2001). The benefits and costs of serious running. *World Leisure Journal*, 43(2), 12–25.

McPherson, B.D., Curtis, J.E., & Loy, J.W. (1989). *The social significance of sport*. Champaign, IL: Human Kinetics.

McQuarrie, F., & Jackson, E.L. (1996). Connections between negotiation of leisure constraints and serious leisure: An exploratory study of adult amateur ice skaters. *Loisir et Société/Society and Leisure*, 19, 459–83.

Mellor, B.E. (2006). Radical shift: A grounded theory approach to midlife career change of professionals. Masters Thesis, Department of Sociology, University of Calgary.

Midlarsky, E., & Kahana, E. (1994). *Altruism in later life*. Thousand Oaks, CA: Sage.

Mitchell, R.G., Jr. (1983). *Mountain experience: The psychology and sociology of adventure*. Chicago, IL: University of Chicago Press.

Musick, M.A., & Wilson, J. (2008). *Volunteers: A social profile*. Bloomington, IN: Indiana University Press.

Nardi, P.M. (1988). The social world of magicians: Gender and conjuring. *Sex Roles*, 19, 759–70.

New World Encyclopedia. (2008). Edutainment. http://www.newworld encyclopedia.org/entry/Edutainment (retrieved 3 March 2012).

New York Times. (2013a). Your first visual arts crush. 14 August (online edition).

New York Times. (2013b). Remembering the spark that ignited a creative fire. 1 September (online edition).

New York Times. (2013c). Your first theater crush. 21 August (online edition).

Olmsted, A.D. (1988). Morally controversial leisure: The social world of the gun collector. *Symbolic Interaction*, 11, 277–87.

Olmsted, A.D. (1991). Collecting: Leisure, investment, or obsession? *Journal of Social Behavior and Personality*, 6, 287–306.

Overs, R.P. (1984). *Guide to avocational activities*. Sussex, WI: Signpost Press.

Pawluk, A. (1984). The status and style of life of polish Olympians after completion of their sports careers. *International Review of Sport Sociology*, 19, 169–83.

Pearce, J.L. (1993). *Volunteers: The organizational behavior of unpaid workers.* New York, NY: Routledge.

Perreault, M. (1988). La passion et le corps comme objets de la sociologie: La danse comme carrière. *Sociologie et Société*, 20, 177–86.

Perry, R., & Carnegie, E. (2013). Reading pro-am theatre through a serious leisure lens: Organisational and policy-making implications. *Leisure Studies*, 32, 383–98.

Pilon, M. (2013). Races end fees to top runners, drawing outcry. *New York Times*, 2 October (online edition).

Ploch, L. (1976). Community development in action: A case study. *Journal of Community Development and Society*, 7, 8.

Prose, F. (2009). *Reading like a writer: A guide for people who love books and for those who want to write them.* New York: HarperCollins.

Puddephatt, A.J. (2005). Advancing in the amateur chess world. In D. Pawluch, W. Shaffir, & C. Miall (Eds.), *Doing ethnography: Studying everyday life* (pp. 300–11). Toronto, ON: Canadian Scholars' Press.

Putnam, R.D. (2000). *Bowling alone: The collapse and revival of American community.* New York: Simon & Schuster.

Regelski, T.A. (2007). Amateuring in music and its rivals. *Action, Criticism, and Theory for Music Education*, 6(3). (retrieved from http://act.maydaygroup.org/index.php).

Reid, D. (1995). *Work and leisure in the 21st century: From production to citizenship.* Toronto: Wall and Emerson.

Rifkin, J. (1995). *The end of work: The decline of the global labor force and the dawn of the post-market era.* New York: G.P. Putnam's Sons.

Ringette/Ringuette Canada. (2012). http://www.ringette.ca/en-us/oursport/history (retrieved 15 September 2012).

Risling, G. (2007). Prescription drugs part of Hollywood. *ABC News Internet Ventures* (retrieved 7 October 2007).

Roberts, K. (1999). *Leisure in contemporary society.* Wallingford, UK: CABI.

Rojek, C. (2002). Civil labour, leisure and post work society. *Loisir et Société/Society and Leisure*, 25, 21–36.

Roncaglia, I. (2010). Retirement transition in ballet dancers: 'Coping within and coping without.' *Qualitative Social Research*, 11(2) (online edition).

Rosenbaum, M.S. (2013). Maintaining the trail: Collective action in a serious-leisure community. *Journal of Contemporary Ethnography*, 42(6), 639–67.

Rosenblum, B. (1978). *Photographers at work: A sociology of photographic styles.* New York: Holmes & Meier.

Routier, G. (2013). Rompre avec le danger: Une analyse sociologique du dégagement corporel. *Loisir et Société/Society and Leisure*, 36, 232–48.

Salamon, E., & Robinson, B.W. (1987). Gender role socialization: A review of the literature. In E. Salamon & B.W. Robinson (Eds.), *Gender roles: Doing what comes naturally.* Toronto, ON: Methuen.

Samuel, N. (1996). Introduction. In N. Samuel (Ed.), *Women, leisure, and the family in contemporary society: A multinational perspective* (pp. 1–14). Wallingford, UK: CABI.

Schein, E.H. (2007). Afterword: Career research – some issues and dilemmas. In H. Gunz & M. Peiperl (Eds.), *Handbook of career studies* (pp. 573–76). Thousand Oaks, CA: Sage.

Scott, D. (2008). Foreword to the 2008 edition. In H. Bryan (Ed.), *Conflict in the great outdoors* (pp. ix–xi). Birmingham, AL: The Birmingham Publishing Company.

Scott, D. (2012). Serious leisure and recreation specialization: An uneasy marriage. *Leisure Sciences*, 34, 366–71.

Scott, D., Ditton, R.B., Stoll, J.R., & Eubanks, T.L. (2005). Measuring specialization among birders: Utility of a self-classification measure. *Human Dimensions of Wildlife*, 10, 53–74.

Scott, D., & Godbey, G.C. (1994). Recreation specialization in the social world of contract bridge. *Journal of Leisure Research*, 26, 275–95.

Seltzer, G. (1989). *Music matters: The performer and the American federation of musicians*. Metuchen, NJ: Scarecrow.

Shen, X.S., & Yarnal, C. (2010). Blowing open the serious leisure-casual leisure dichotomy: What's in there? *Leisure Sciences*, 32, 162–79.

Siegenthaler, K.L., & O'Dell, I. (2003). Older golfers: Serious leisure and successful aging. *World Leisure Journal*, 45(1), 45–52.

Simpson, C.R. (1981). *SoHo: The artist in the city*. Chicago: University of Chicago Press.

Sinha, A. (1979). Control in craft work: The case of production potters. *Qualitative Sociology*, 2, 3–25.

Smith, D.H., Stebbins, R.A., & Dover, M. (2006). *A dictionary of nonprofit terms and concepts*. Bloomington, IN: Indiana University Press.

Spence, R. (2013). Do you have what it takes to run your own business? *Financial Post*, Friday, 1 March (online edition).

Stalp, M.C. (2007). *Quilting: The fabric of everyday life*. New York: Berg.

Statistics Canada (2001). Caring Canadians, involved Canadians: Highlights from the 2000 national survey of giving, volunteering, and participating (cat. No. 71-542-XIE). Ottawa, ON: Ministry of Industry, Government of Canada.

Stebbins, R.A. (1962). The conflict between musical and commercial values in the Minneapolis jazz community. *Proceedings of the Minnesota Academy of Science*, 30, 75–9.

Stebbins, R.A. (1970). Career: The subjective approach. *The Sociological Quarterly*, 11, 32–49.

Stebbins, R.A. (1978). Classical music amateurs: A definitional study. *Humboldt Journal of Social Relations*, 5(Spring-Summer), 78–103.

Stebbins, R.A. (1979). *Amateurs: On the margin between work and leisure*. Beverly Hills, CA: Sage (also available at www.seriousleisure.net/Digital Library).

Stebbins, R.A. (1980). Avocational science: The amateur routine in archaeology and astronomy. *International Journal of Comparative Sociology*, 21(March-June), 34–48.

Stebbins, R.A. (1981). Science amators? Rewards and costs in amateur astronomy and archaeology. *Journal of Leisure Research*, 13, 289–304.

Stebbins, R.A. (1982). Serious leisure: A conceptual statement. *Pacific Sociological Review*, 25, 251–72.

Stebbins, R.A. (1990). *The laugh-makers: Stand-up comedy as art, business, and life-style.* Montréal, QC and Kingston, ON: McGill-Queen's University Press.

Stebbins, R.A. (1992). *Amateurs, professionals, and serious leisure.* Montreal, QC and Kingston, ON: McGill-Queen's University Press.

Stebbins, R.A. (1993a). *Canadian football: A view from the helmet* (reprinted edition with new Introduction). Toronto, ON: Canadian Scholars Press.

Stebbins, R.A. (1993b). *Career, culture and social psychology in a variety art: The magician* (reprinted edition). Malabar, FL: Krieger.

Stebbins, R.A. (1994). The liberal arts hobbies: A neglected subtype of serious leisure. *Loisir et Société/Society and Leisure*, 16, 173–86.

Stebbins, R.A. (1995). Leisure and selfishness: An exploration. In G.S. Fain (Ed.), *Reflections on the philosophy of leisure, Vol. II, Leisure and ethics* (pp. 292–303). Reston, VA: American Alliance for Health, Physical Education, Recreation, and Dance.

Stebbins, R.A. (1996a). *The barbershop singer: Inside the social world of a musical hobby.* Toronto, ON: University of Toronto Press.

Stebbins, R.A. (1996b). Volunteering: A serious leisure perspective. *Nonprofit and Voluntary Action Quarterly*, 25, 211–24.

Stebbins, R.A. (1997). Casual leisure: A conceptual statement. *Leisure Studies* 16, 17–25.

Stebbins, R.A. (2000). The extraprofessional life: Leisure, retirement, and unemployment. *Current Sociology*, 48 (2000), 1–27.

Stebbins, R. A. (2001a). *Exploratory research in the social sciences.* Thousand Oaks, CA: Sage.

Stebbins, R.A. (2001b). Volunteering – mainstream and marginal: Preserving the leisure experience. In M. Graham & M. Foley (Eds.), *Volunteering in leisure: Marginal or inclusive?* (LSA Publication No. 75), pp. 1–10. Eastbourne, UK: Leisure Studies Association.

Stebbins, R.A. (2002). *The organizational basis of leisure participation: A motivational exploration.* State College, PA: Venture.

Stebbins, R.A. (2004a). Fun, enjoyable, satisfying, fulfilling: Describing positive leisure experience. *Leisure Studies Association Newsletter* 69(November), 8–11. (Also available at www.seriousleisure.net/Digital Library, Reflections 7).

Stebbins, R.A. (2004b). Stamp collecting. In G.S. Cross (Ed.), *Encyclopedia of recreation and leisure in America* (pp. 310–11). New York: Charles Scribners' Sons.

Stebbins, R.A. (2004c/2014). *Between work and leisure: The common ground of two separate worlds.* New Brunswick, NJ: Transaction Publishers (paperback edition with new Preface, 2014).

Stebbins, R.A. (2004d). Pleasurable aerobic activity: A type of casual leisure with salubrious implications. *World Leisure Journal*, 46(4), 55–8 (also available at www.seriousleisure.net/ Digital Library/Other Works).

Stebbins, R.A. (2005a). *Challenging mountain nature: Risk, motive, and lifestyle in three hobbyist sports.* Calgary, AB: Detselig. (Also available at www. seriousleisure.net/Digital Library).

Stebbins, R.A. (2005b). Project-based leisure: Theoretical neglect of a common use of free time. *Leisure Studies*, 24, 1–11.

Stebbins, R.A. (2005c). Serious leisure, recreational specialization, and complex leisure activity. *Leisure Studies Association Newsletter*, 70 (March), pp. 11–13. Also available at www.seriousleisure.net/ Digital Library, 'Leisure Reflections No.8'.

Stebbins, R.A. (2006). Mentoring as a leisure activity: On the informal world of small-scale altruism. *World Leisure Journal*, 48(4), 3–10.

Stebbins, R.A. (2007a). A leisure-based, theoretic typology of volunteers and volunteering. *Leisure Studies Association Newsletter*, 78, November, 9–12 (also available at www.seriousleisure.net/Digital Library, 'Leisure Reflections No.16').

Stebbins, R.A. (2007b). *Serious leisure: A perspective for our time.* New Brunswick, NJ: Transaction.

Stebbins, R.A. (2008). Leisure abandonment: Quitting free time activity that we love. *Leisure Studies Association Newsletter*, 81 (2008, November): 14–19. Also available at www.seriousleisure.net/Digital Library, "Leisure Reflections No.19."

Stebbins, R.A. (2010). Addiction to work and leisure activities: Is it possible? *Leisure Studies Association Newsletter*, 86 (July), 19–22 (also available at www. seriousleisure.net/Digital Library, 'Leisure Reflections No. 24').

Stebbins, R.A. (2012a). *The idea of leisure: First principles.* New Brunswick, NJ: Transaction.

Stebbins, R.A. (2012b). Comment on Scott: Recreation specialization and the CL-SL continuum. *Leisure Sciences*, 34, 372–4.

Stebbins, R.A. (2013a). Unpaid work of love: Defining the work-leisure axis of volunteering. *Leisure Studies*, 32, 339–45.

Stebbins, R.A. (2013b). *The committed reader: Reading for utility, pleasure and fulfillment in the twenty-first century.* Lanham, MD: Scarecrow.

Stebbins, R.A. (2013c). *Planning your time in retirement: How to cultivate a leisure lifestyle to suit your needs and interests.* Lanham, MD: Rowman & Littlefield.

Stebbins, R.A. (2014). Experience as knowledge: Its place in leisure. *Leisure Studies Association Newsletter*, 98 (July), XXXX (also available at www. seriousleisure.net/Digital Library, 'Leisure Reflections No. 36').

Stiers, J. (2007). Game, name and fame – afterwards, will I still be the same? A social psychological study of career, role exit and identity. *International Review for the Sociology of Sport*, 42, 99–111.

Styles, C. (2007). Library-based adult reading for pleasure in the USA and the Netherlands: Transferable lessons for English public libraries (source: http://www.cloreleadership.org/~clorelea/cms/user_files/fellow_fellowship_research_projects_download_report/33/Claire%20Styles%20Clore%20Research%202007.pdf, retrieved 18 December 2011).

Sulcas, R. (2007). Often a swan, rarely a queen. *New York Times*, 16 December (online edition).

Sutherland, D.E. (1989). Ballet as a career. In A.W. Foster & J.R. Blau (Eds.), *Art and society*. Albany, NY: State University of New York Press.

Theberge, N. (1977). An occupational analysis of women's professional golf. PhD Dissertation, Department of Sociology, University of Massachusetts, Amherst, MA.

Theberge, N. (1980). The system of rewards in women's professional golf. *International Review of Sport Sociology*, 15(2), 27–42.

Thomson, K. (2013). Roles, revenue, and responsibilities: The changing nature of being a working musician. *Work and Occupations*, 40, 514–25.

Tommasini, A. (2013). It all started with a toy piano. *New York Times*, 17 July 2013, online edition.

Toneguzzi, M. (2012). Refinishing hobby now lucrative business. *Calgary Herald*, Monday, 14 May, p. B3.

Toneguzzi, M. (2013). Passion for jewelry and art grows into business venture. *Calgary Herald*, Monday, 18 February, p. B4.

Trimbur, L. (2013). *Come out swinging: The changing world of boxing in Gleason's gym*. Princeton, NJ: Princeton University Press.

Tsaur, S.-H., & Liang, T.-W. (2008). Serious leisure and recreation specialization. *Leisure Sciences*, 30, 325–41.

Unruh, D.R. (1980). The nature of social worlds. *Pacific Sociological Review*, 23, 271–96.

Waddington, I. (2000). Sports and health: A sociological perspective. In J. Coakley & E. Dunning (Eds.), *Handbook of sports studies* (pp. 408–21). Thousand Oaks, CA: Sage.

Wakin, D. (2007). See you at the barre. *New York Times*, 23 March 2007 (Retrieved 31 March 2013, http://www.nytimes.com/2007/03/23/arts/dance/23ball.html?pagewanted=all&_r=0).

Walker, G.J., & Fenton, L. (2013). Backgrounds of, and factors affecting, highly productive leisure researchers. *Journal of Leisure Research*, 45, 537–62.

Westby, D.L. (1960). The career experience of the symphony musician. *Social Forces* 38, 223–30.

Williams, C.C., Nadin, S., & Rodgers, P. (2012). Evaluating competing theories of informal entrepreneurship: Some lessons from Ukraine. *International Journal of Entrepreneurial Behaviour & Research*, 18(5), 528–43.

Index

Note: Locators followed by 'n' refer to notes.

Printed and bound by CPI Group (UK) Ltd, Croydon, CR0 4YY